Writing Personal

Notes & Letters

Compliments of
JACKSON'S
THE LEADING CASH
Tea, Coffee and Confectionery Store,
272 River St. Troy, N. Y.

Writing Personal

Notes & Letters

JENNIFER WILLIAMS

And the Editors of
Victoria *Magazine*

Hearst Books • A Division of Sterling Publishing Co., Inc.
New York

Library of Congress Cataloging-in-Publication Data
Available upon request.

10   9   8   7   6   5   4   3   2   1

Published by Hearst Books,
A Division of Sterling Publishing Co., Inc.
387 Park Avenue South, New York, N.Y. 10016

www.victoriamag.com

Distributed in Canada by Sterling Publishing
℅ Canadian Manda Group, One Atlantic Avenue, Suite 105
Toronto, Ontario, Canada M6K 3E7
Distributed in Australia by Capricorn Link (Australia) Pty. Ltd.
P.O. Box 704, Windsor, NSW 2756 Australia

Manufactured in China

ISBN 1-58816-195-1

Foreword

A beautiful letter is a treasure. And all of us have friends whose name above the return address makes our hearts beat a little faster. When my friend Martha writes, her prose is graceful, and I feel better for having read about her trip to Wales or her poetry studies. Good letter-writers are correspondents, not unlike journalists, really.

In this volume, we have given you good letters to enjoy and to inspire your own writing. Judy just wrote me about her family's new careers, and it got me thinking about how these gracious people are growing. Not only did I take satisfaction in the story but I began to think about my own life a bit differently.

My in-laws fell in love through a cross-continental correspondence. Their marriage proved to be long and wonderful, perhaps made better because so many thoughts were carefully expressed before vows were taken.

Each of you will, I hope, consider writing more often, taking it as a privilege rather than a duty. Even business is better done when expressed eloquently. If you treasure the letters you receive, become a writer giving the same joy to others.

NANCY LINDEMEYER
Founding Editor
Victoria Magazine

Contents

Distributed by Royal Specialty Sales, 430 K

Introduction

While she was still very young, Anne Morrow Lindbergh made a wonderfully perceptive observation in her diary about herself, her mother, and letter-writing: "We have never talked together the way we have sometimes in letters. Why do I meet people better in letters?" Perhaps the answer to Lindbergh's question is revealed in the question itself. The best letters are always about meaningful "meeting." Even the earliest ones illustrate our desire to reveal and share the rich and varied load of everyday experience, whether it is played out at home or at the very heart of public life. Of course, the more personal the letter, the more it appeals to the spirit of meeting.

If, in centuries earlier than ours, many letters were written out of practical necessity, a great many more were written out of desire. Women in particular made the medium their own, perhaps because they had so few other outlets for personal expression. Through letters women funneled all the force and fervor of their thoughts, affections, wisdom, and concern for others. Our letters nourished friendships and family ties despite incredible separations by distance, marriage, politics, and war. Letters formed a bulwark against loneliness and isolation when there were few distractions from the hard realities of everyday life. Letters kept us informed before newspapers were widely circulated and told us about distant places before most people had the means to travel. When there was little psychological or legal counsel to be had, letters filled in the gaps with advice and comfort. Letters kept us in touch with the world and gave us a lasting sense of connection to one another. They still do, even if letters have a slightly different look these days.

By the eighteenth century, no education was considered complete without a thorough understanding of the mechanics and esthetics of correspondence. But for those who really practice it, the art of letter-writing has always been more than a means to an end. Indeed, for someone as fiercely passionate as Madame de Sévigné, writing letters was a reason for being. In 1671 she began what would eventually become a famous twenty-five-year correspondence with her daughter, the Countess de Grignan. For Madame de Sévigné, writing to her daughter was "the first order of business"; it took precedence over everything in her life. "My God," she once wrote, "how eagerly I await your letters! It's been almost an hour already since I received one!"

The pleasure of sharing ourselves is no less important now than it ever was. A letter that takes only ten minutes to write can have tremendous immediacy and give the person who receives it an exhilarating sense of "being there," next to you, living in the same moment with you.

Unlike most telephone conversations, a letter gives us time to reflect and compose our thoughts without interruption or distraction. In letters we can watch each other's lives unfold, moment by moment.

There's nothing like a letter to capture precious moments, especially today when we take so little time to relish them. Recently there's been a groundswell of interest in bringing back small personal touches that say "you matter to me." Something as simple as writing an invitation by hand or sending a thank-you note to a friend for a special dinner or a wonderful weekend may not seem significant at all in the larger scheme of things, but it is a compelling sign, nonetheless, that the human hand is an enduring source of beauty and illumination in an increasingly mechanical and impersonal world.

But even the most habitual letter-writers sometimes find it difficult to write a condolence letter or a thank-you note. Hopefully, this book will help you discover ways of feeling confident—and even inspired—every time you sit down, no matter what the purpose of your letter.

In the end, writing a letter is an adventure to be embarked upon with a happy, expectant heart. It will give your life more joy and meaning than you can imagine. So, go quickly! Write a letter now, even if it's just a few lines to propose a picnic, relate a dream, or share a sudden thought, joke, inspiration, or memory. Write to say hello, and I'm thinking of you. Write to say I hope you're feeling better. Write to say it's raining and cozy by the lamplight and I miss you. Just write, and wait: An enchanting letter will soon be on its way to you. . . .

I have now attained the true art of letter-writing, which, we are always told, is to express on paper exactly what one would say to the same person by word of mouth; I have been talking to you almost as fast as I could the whole of this letter.

Jane Austen to her sister, Cassandra

chapter one

POST CARD

This side for Correspondence.

This side for Address.

NEW ORLEANS, LA
AUG 5
12 30 PM
1907

The Pleasures of Staying in Touch

A Meditation on Letter-Writing

A friend says she spent her entire childhood waiting for letters in the cavernous lobby of an apartment building on Riverside Drive. It was a magical place despite drafts and strange echoes, for every day—usually after one o'clock in the afternoon—the mailman would materialize at the front door, just like a genie from a bottle. With him came the incomparable mysteries of the mailbag. Nothing, she says, will ever rival the almost intolerable sense of anticipation and pleasure she felt each time the postman dipped his hand into the bag: "Is there anything for me?"

And sure enough, tucked between the glossy pages of *National Geographic* or *Life,* there might be a little square of dove-colored paper from her grandmother in Denver, or a powder-blue envelope

It is cold tonight, but the

thought of you so warm,

that I sit by it as a fireside,

and am never cold any more.

I love to write to you—

It gives my heart a holiday

and sets the bells to ringing.

Emily Dickinson

with a kitten on it from her friend Betsy, who was at camp in Maine and had the measles. One time there was even a postcard with a tiny bag of sand attached to it. On the front it said, "Greetings from Miami Beach," and on the back there was a funny message from her father, who was on a business trip in Florida and sounded a little lonely for home. Decades later, the postcard and its small, unopened bag of sand still have the power to enchant.

It's curious how emblematic a single letter can be, how it can encapsulate an era or sum up a complex relationship.

The beauty of being written to is the sense of importance it gives us. It is immensely pleasing and flattering to be singled out and acknowledged as someone worthy of a letter. Just the other day a good friend's eight-year-old daughter received her first letter from a schoolmate. She was so thrilled and happy to see her own name—and no one else's—on a pink envelope, sealed with purple wax, and with a real stamp on it, that she simply couldn't put it down all evening. It's easy to see how this luxurious feeling can become addictive; but the satisfactions of a letter-writing habit only deepen with time.

As teenagers, many of us were fervid, if not always happy, letter-writers, especially after the differences between ourselves and our parents had become all too obvious. The letters we exchanged with friends, however, created a private world of shared values, grievances, passions, and hopes; they sustained us during the most tumultuous years of our physical growth and encouraged the development of a rich interior life. Letters gave us something to look forward to when we weren't cramming for exams or hiding from the world because of a new set of braces, or, worse, the ghastly overnight discovery that one had grown taller—and would always be taller—than the tallest boy in our class: "Dear Harriet, I could kill myself. Eddie Wolfe is four feet shorter than I am. . . . "

The heartfelt letters we write as teenagers eventually evolve into more mature forms of correspondence: love letters that burst with borrowed phrases from Browning and Shakespeare; and long pensive letters to college buddies or friends at home. During these years, personal writing of any kind, whether it's in a diary or a letter, gratifies our need for intimacy and, at the same time, gives us a satisfying outlet for self-expression. There's something forgiving about a letter: Budding writers know that it's a safe place to stretch.

It's amazing how quickly our status at home changes once we've gone into the world. . . . Although, come to think of it, the transition isn't always so smooth. Some parents might be inclined to acknowledge their children's independence and level-headedness—but most don't: F. Scott Fitzgerald wrote plenty of funny and literary letters to his daughter, Scottie, while she was away at college, but even he couldn't resist serving up a little old-

I have just re-read your letter and now my head aches with a kind of sweet excitement. Do you know what I mean? It is what a little girl feels when she has been put to bed at the end of a long sunny day and still sees upon her closed eyelids the image of dancing boughs and flowery bushes.

Katherine Mansfield to Bertrand Russ

fashioned parental advice: "Take care of yourself mentally (study when you're fresh), physically (don't pluck your eyebrows), morally (don't get where you have to lie). . . . "

These days, it's a little alarming to discover just how much our letters to our own children sound like the ones our parents wrote to us. But the strange and lovely thing is that we probably don't mind. It's a relief and a pleasure to realize, at last, that we have the freedom to write to our parents with the same ease and candor we bring to other friendly letters. In fact, some of the best letters are exchanged between adult children and their parents. George Eliot, William Faulkner, Anne Morrow Lindbergh, Isak Dinesen, and Sylvia Plath wrote as movingly to their mothers as Lord Chesterfield, Madame de Sévigné, and Anna Akhmatova wrote to their children. No matter when or under what circumstances these letters were written, one can always find something deeply familiar and true in them: "There is so little time to say things," Anne Morrow Lindbergh observed in a letter to her mother. "I am always putting away things that are too real to say, and then they never get said. We are always bargaining with our feelings so that we can live from day to day."

With so much hurry and pressure in our lives, we sometimes forget that it's perfectly all right to slow down and take pleasure in what we do. "I write letters for myself," a friend admitted recently, "because it makes me feel good. I could spend the time doing all the things I *should* be doing, like defrosting the refrigerator, but I'd rather sit down, calmly, and try to connect with someone I care about, someone I don't want to lose in the busy bustle of things."

Another friend always keeps a big, untidy box full of beautiful papers, unusual cards, pens, and photographs on hand. Between leaving work and picking up her children from school, she always carves out half an hour to do something she looks forward to all day: "Writing a letter, even if it's a short one, makes me feel as if I have a life," she says. "I adore my children and my work, but the world is very big—and I want to stay in touch with my friends, my mother, my cousins in Toronto. . . . " A phone call might very well do the trick for someone else, but for her, real connection comes down to a focused, thoughtful effort. "Letter-writing energizes me, too," she says, "because it wakes me up and gets my creative juices flowing again. I feel like myself when I'm writing."

Horace Walpole once said, "I never understand anything until I have written about it." Letters really are windows on the soul. The meatiest and most interesting ones are full of self-discovery.

Whoever said that letters are the most immediate form of autobiography was right. Every time you "canter out on paper," as Virginia Woolf put it, you add a new chapter to the story of your life. Although it is true that letters commemorate, document, and

As to making any adequate return for such a letter as yours, my dearest Fanny, it is absolutely impossible, if I were to labour at it all the rest of my life and live to the age of Methuselah, I could never accomplish anything so long and so perfect.

Jane Austen to Fanny Knight

enlarge the most important passages in our lives—births, weddings, deaths—it's the odd detail we tend to remember and communicate, something specific that perfectly reveals the essence of a place or describes the texture of a mood or a moment. In their letters, Madame de Sévigné, Colette, Jane Austen, and Virginia Woolf often luxuriate in pleasurable and sensual moments: eating buttered bread and violets; swimming in a "coppery pink" sea; drinking wine on a sofa near the fire; or sitting "in hot sunshine on the doorstep of a Roman ruin . . . "

It is very gratifying to be let into someone else's life, to be entrusted with the soft, small moments as well as the more imposing ones. But it is also pleasing to unfold the supple fabric of your own experience. A written life has extra intensity: Individual moments seem as fixed and luminous as the images in a particularly memorable photograph.

The truth is we don't have time to worry about making mistakes, especially not in letters, where there is all the freedom in the world to be yourself. F. Scott Fitzgerald said, "All good writing is swimming under water and holding your breath." A letter doesn't have to conform to any particular set of rules. In fact, the more fluid it is the better. Half the pleasure of writing a letter is sharing the moment as it unfolds, impressing it with your mood and the quicksilver shape of your thoughts.

Travel very often throws personality into sharp relief. When we write about another landscape or a culture different from our own, we reveal a little more about ourselves. At the very least, a letter gives us the freedom to express our opinions honestly. When Colette visited Italy in the fall of 1910, she grumbled to her friend Léon Hamel that the weather was deplorable. Worse yet, she wrote, the famous ruins at Herculaneum had left her utterly cold. Italy really wasn't for her, she concluded, despite its delicious gardens and the fragrant torch-lit Grotto of the Sibyl.

Byron observed that "one of the pleasures of reading old letters is the knowledge that they need no answer." It's true that writing a letter requires a little effort—certainly more than picking up the telephone or hanging over the garden wall for a long chat—but to letter-writers, writing is an indispensable act of friendship. There's nothing passive about sitting down to write a letter at all! In fact, it's an extremely vigorous way of saying, "I'm thinking of you"— which is, after all, the premise of any letter. Writing deepens and broadens that sentiment; it exercises your mind and imagination, and gives you an excuse to be as playful, earnest, loving, or moody as you like.

Time and effort are hardly issues to be reckoned with at all, when you think of the advantages of staying in touch. More than the tele-phone, or any other time-saving form of communication, letter-writing maintains friendships uninterrupted over the course of a lifetime: It gives us the comforting sense that our lives are shared. Samuel Johnson once quipped that at the very least a letter "shows one not to be forgotten." But there is much matter in what he said. Letters do keep our friendships from languishing—even a postcard sent on the run or a note written in the half light of a café or a seat on a train can rekindle the spark.

The telephone is so much a part of our lives—at work and at home—that it feels wonderful to take a break from

PRIORITAIRE
1:a-klassbrev

it on occasion. It is astonishing how much you can accomplish without phone interruptions, especially the "junk" calls—recorded ads and solicitations for money—and calls from people you'd prefer not to talk to, at least not right now. A letter is never as strident or insistent as a telephone; it has lovely manners and quietly waits on the mantel or kitchen table until the moment is right for you to hear its message.

Some things can be very awkward to say over the telephone, but a letter gives you time to compose your thoughts calmly and a place to express them completely. It sounds paradoxical, but sometimes a little distance can actually help you get closer to the things you want to say. "I tend to bungle important conversations if I have them over the phone," a friend admits. "I get distracted by something the other person says and lose concentration. I end up talking in circles for hours. When I hang up I always feel like calling back again to say all the things I meant to say but didn't."

A letter takes into account the person to whom you are writing. It gives him or her time to digest what you have said without interruption or embarrassment: "Thanks for the note," another friend recently wrote. "It cleared up the feeling that you hadn't heard me."

There has been a lot of public conversation about reducing the amount of noise, speed, and clutter in everyday life, and "getting back" to doing the things that lift our spirits and nourish our souls. Writing letters immerses us in a quiet, calming mood that allows us to enjoy all the pleasures of solitude while feeling connected to other people.

Letter-writing is a particularly soothing and approachable form of human connection, especially these days, when everyone seems to be looking for faster computers. What we generally need most, however, is something that can help us slow down and decompress. Letter-writing can help you discover what some people refer to as "the quiet center." Writing has a meditative effect that gives everyone access to the rich and revitalizing products of a well-stocked inner life. It is easier to discover what you really think, feel, and wish to communicate if you allow yourself to slow down, take a deep breath, and dip into your own quiet center.

What cannot letters inspire? They have souls; they can speak; they have in them all that force which expresses the transports of the heart; they have all the fire of our passions, they can raise them as much as if the persons themselves were present; they have all the tenderness and the delicacy of speech, and sometimes even a boldness of expression beyond it.

Héloïse to Abel

Staying on top of the communications scene is compelling, but it can also be exhausting and, at times, impersonal. Electronic mail isn't the most private form of communication, either, despite its conveniences, but it's here to stay, along with the Internet and World Wide Web. Technology has given us endless possibilities for meaningful connection, and yet without a decent three-way adapter, there's not much use for it.

There was a wonderful article in *The New York Times* a while back about a woman who took all the latest computer equipment on a trip to Tibet, only to discover, after she'd arrived, that her hardware was more of an inconvenience than a boon. It would be silly to suggest even for a moment that we should go back to scratchy quill pens and messy inkpots to say the things we want to say to each other, but the point of the Tibet story was that great pleasures can be derived from a more direct approach to the world and how we experience it. After her electronic equipment failed, the traveler to Tibet could still enjoy the satisfactions of pen and paper. In the end, the act of writing itself fostered a state of mind that was ultimately more compatible with the landscape, culture, and spirit of the place.

You can write a letter anywhere—sitting on a bench on the boardwalk at Coney Island or perched on the Great Wall of China. No special equipment is necessary. Some of the world's most memorable letters are written at home. Edith Wharton, Mark Twain,

Winston Churchill, and Marcel Proust wrote in bed. The prolific Madame de Sévigné wrote enchanting letters from a seat by her own hearth; and Jane Austen, another habitual letter-writer and frequent houseguest, managed to compose perfectly entertaining letters, even if she had only half an hour before breakfast to do it ("very snug, in my own room, lovely morning, excellent fire, fancy me"). Letter-writing is something you can do any way you like, wherever you like. It is a completely individual effort—private, intimate, unlike anything else. In the end, what you create is a small but inimitable work of art, something someone you love can hold in their hands and treasure for a lifetime.

Is it too fanciful to say that a letter is magical? Just think of it for a moment: A letter has the feel of something as everyday as your hat or a soup ladle, yet it can move as softly and swiftly as fog across great distances. A letter is as fluid as any stream that carves stone, and yet, after all of its various transformations, it eventually lands on your kitchen table, solid as a teapot. But letters aren't all fancy. The pleasures they offer are exquisitely tangible. In her novel *Villette,* Charlotte Brontë's scrappy heroine Lucy Snowe perfectly describes the experience of possessing and consuming a letter:

It felt, not flimsy, but firm, substantial, satisfying. . . . I held in my hand a morsel of real solid joy: not a dream, not an image of the brain. . . . It was neither sweet hail, nor small coriander-seed—neither slight wafer, nor luscious honey . . . it was the wild savoury mess of the hunter, nourishing and salubrious meat, forest-fed or desert-reared, fresh, healthful, and life-sustaining.

Letters support our lives in all kinds of ways: Madame de Sévigné's correspondence with her daughter, Madame de Grignan, was mutually nourishing; Emily Dickinson's letters conveyed her poetry to the world; and for Jane Austen, who wrote regularly to her sister, Cassandra, letters were the building blocks of a coherent family life.

One of the most revealing moments in *Villette* occurs when Lucy Snowe suddenly realizes why Dr. John's letter has made her so intensely happy: He wrote it "not merely to content me—but to gratify *himself.*" Perhaps Lucy stumbled on the motivating force behind the writing of all good letters: the desire to please yourself and, at the same time, make someone else feel happy. "Is it possible that my letters are as pleasing to you as you tell me they are?" Madame de Sévigné asked her daughter. "Is it possible that I write so well? I write so fast! But if you are pleased I ask no more!"

Just knowing that someone else loves reading your letters can inspire you to keep writing them, even if you receive very few in return. A friend who has two very active little boys rarely has time to write, but when she does she always expresses her appreciation:

Your letters often have the effect of several bracing cups of coffee on days when I can barely pick up my feet. I always intend to write back to you but end up

It is impossible, totally impossible, my dearest daughter, for me to express to you the joy I felt on opening that blessed packet of mail which brought me news of your safe delivery. . . . What do you think a person does in a moment of such extreme joyousness? Do you know what happens? One feels one's heart constrict and one weeps uncontrollably. That is what I did, my dearest daughter, and did it with great pleasure.

Madame de Sévigné

loading the washer or changing diapers instead. After the boys are in bed I col-
lapse. Thank you for keeping the faith and writing so many marvelous letters.
I hope you know that you are always in my thoughts, despite the silence from
this end.

The pleasures of receiving letters are all too obvious, but one might be tempted to ask, who has the time to write them? The fact is, there is always time to do the things you want to do. It's just a matter of deciding what's important. A letter shows that you've chosen to make friendship a priority, and that you're not too busy to care, whether it's a note to a neighbor who has been recently hospitalized; a thank-you note to a good friend for a wonderful dinner; or a long, thoughtful letter to a younger sister who needs encouragement.

Letters are a gift of your time and affection, which makes them very rare and special, but they also give back a great deal to the writer. A close friend says she feels "cleansed" after writing a good letter: "It's better than therapy," she says. "Afterward I feel light and happy because I feel as if I've done something important and good for someone else." When writing is this satisfying, it's hard not to find the time for letters. After all, what could be more important than staying in touch with the people you care about most?

The good news is that we are actually writing to each other more than ever. Electronic mail has given us the freedom to write as quickly and informally as we like, without fuss and with no need for stationery, pens, or stamps. Still, the main focus of E-mail is function over form: to transmit a message with alacrity—not to produce subtle or memorable correspondence. A friend admits that she loves E-mail, but is quick to add that "it's not the same as getting a letter. I use electronic mail as a convenience, I'm completely hooked on it, but I still hold my breath every time I open my mailbox. I feel let down if there are no personal letters."

Letter-writing is not a lost art. If anything, the spirit, and most certainly the accoutrements, of letter-writing—fountain pens, sealing waxes, scented inks, luxurious papers, and even calligraphy—are making a comeback! Despite everything, we still yearn to be personal, to share personal feelings, and have a personal style. Privacy means more to us than ever, now that almost anyone with a modicum of computer savvy can access our most personal files. In the cool, public world of electronic media, a letter still exudes the warm scent of unassailable privacy.

Electronic mail has many advantages, but there is something disturbingly ephemeral about it. Is it possible that on some deeply human level, we find it distressing to watch any of the important messages we send each other become reduced to a blip on a computer screen? A letter, on the other hand, is a good deal less disposable: At the same time, a letter is risky. E-mail correspondence tends to be far less personal than most correspondence because it is so public. Loss of intimacy is the price we pay, ultimately, for the convenience of speed. It takes courage and time to make a lasting commitment to friendship. Letters are articles of faith and acts of grace: They show that we have made ourselves vulnerable in an effort to share perhaps the deepest part of ourselves with somebody else

Writing Tools

Even after typewriters had become universal, many people still chose to write by hand, perhaps because typewritten letters were generally associated (and sometimes confused) with business correspondence. These days it is a matter of personal style whether you word-process, type, or write a letter, although it is usually best to write thank-you notes, informal invitations and, especially, condolence letters by hand. If your writing is truly illegible, it is perfectly acceptable to type or word-process personal letters, as long as your signature is handwritten.

It is always a courtesy to sign preprinted or embossed Christmas cards: Even a couple of handwritten lines can make all the difference between an impersonal note and a warm, memorable one. This is especially true of "group letters."

One of the most enjoyable aspects of corresponding is indulging one's passion for beautiful writing materials. Happily, most stationers offer a stunning variety of papers, envelopes, pens, scented inks, and sealing waxes from which to choose. Even fountain pens are making a comeback these days—perhaps because they suggest an earlier, more romantic era, when people took the time to pour their hearts and minds into their letters. We still do, of course, and the lovely thing is that we have even more choices now with which to express ourselves through a rich variety of materials, not all of which are store-bought: A friend, for example, makes delicately beautiful papers by hand and imbues each one with an evocative floral or citrus fragrance; another writes in a flowing hand over the soft shades and shapes of her own watercolors; and still another friend creates magnificent cards from lush layers of vintage Victorian papers, heirloom lace, antique buttons, velvet ribbons, and perfectly preserved flowers.

Sealing wax is making a comeback these days, too, but unfortunately it sometimes gets crushed at the post office during mechanical processing. But there are so many other ways of individualizing letters: Some writers choose irregular sheets of paper and unusually large envelopes for their correspondence, and even send letters rolled up in decorative tubes, bottles, or boxes. Others use their favorite scent to leave a redolent imprint of themselves on the page, or send delightfully spontaneous notes on paper torn from a notebook, journal, or sketchpad.

Embossing and engraving are excellent, if more traditional, ways to individualize stationery, and, certainly, if you have a family crest, it too can be used to give letters a personal touch.

Ultimately, it doesn't matter in the least if the letter-writing materials you favor are plain or fancy, innovative or traditional: The main thing is to connect with friends and family in a way that feels right for you.

There are a few occasions, however, that require an especially careful choice of writing materials. For example, it is best to use plain white, ivory, light blue, or gray stationery (or notecards) for condolence letters, thank-you notes, and replies to formal and informal invitations. As for most kinds of business correspondence, it is customary to send a typed letter on plain white or ivory standard-size (8½" × 11") paper, with a matching envelope.

Thankfully, it requires no effort at all to come up with an affectionate ending for a letter to someone close to your heart: Simply seal it "With love," or "With all my love." Informal letters to relatives and friends might also end with Affectionately, Affectionately yours, or With much fondness; but it can sometimes be a little tricky to know how to close a very formal letter, for example, a condolence letter to the family of a friend who has died, or a letter addressed to an elected official, such as a state senator or congresswoman. On these occasions, any of these endings will serve: Respectfully yours, Yours respectfully, Very truly yours, Yours truly.

A less formal letter might close with: Cordially, Cordially yours, Sincerely, Sincerely yours, Yours very sincerely, Always sincerely yours, As ever, Ever yours, Always yours, and so on.

Dear Jennie,

Can you believe it? I'm halfway through the best thing I've ever painted, I think. But I've stopped for now. I need to rest my eyes and refresh my spirits with a cold swim and a glass of beer. Last night I lost my glasses when I plunged off the dock into the sea, which probably accounts for the "impressionistic" breakthrough I think I've made. . . .

August has never been hotter. Not a leaf is stirring and I swear you can hear the sap flowing in the pines. There's an outdoor shower by the side of the house that's full of lizards and a spider with such an intelligent face I can't bear to sweep it out. I never want to sleep in my own bed again—not if I can camp out under these old yews and sniff the sea all night. When I wake up I feel like working right away. The color of the air changes so quickly.

I wish you were here. . . . But you'd leave me in no time at all—the hill on the other side of the inlet is black, black I tell you, with blueberries, and there's a place two miles down the road where they play bluegrass 'til all hours and the beer is cheap and good. Still, if you came maybe you could dive for my lost glasses.

Love, Nina

chapter two

ST CARD

ONLY   FOR THE ADDRESS ONLY

1912

Pictures of the Heart

Letters to Friends

You are inimitable, irresistible. You are the delight of my life. Such letters, such entertaining letters, as you have lately sent!—such a description of your queer little heart!—such a lovely display of what imagination does. You are worth your weight in gold, or even in the new silver coinage. I cannot express to you what I have felt in reading your history of yourself, how full of pity and concern and admiration and amusement I have been. You are the paragon of all that is silly and sensible, common-place and eccentric, sad and lively, provoking and interesting. . . . You are so odd!—and all the time, so perfectly natural—so peculiar in yourself, and yet so like everybody else!

It is very, very gratifying to me to know you so intimately. You can hardly think what a pleasure it is to me, to have such thorough pictures of your heart.

Jane Austen to her niece Fanny Knight

More than any other medium, letters still have the power to enchant, perhaps because each one is written with a single reader in mind. Is it any wonder that so many of us are passionate about letters and the life we live in them, even now, when personal connections can be made instantaneously over the telephone or computer? The time and care lavished on each word and paragraph is a deeply touching act of friendship, especially these days when we seem to have so little time and so many absorbing cares. It is hard to imagine what could be more intimate than a letter, or what might possibly give us a greater sense of importance—of being thought of and trusted—than a letter written just for us.

"A letter always feels to me like immortality because it is the mind alone without corporeal friend," Emily Dickinson once said. To her, there seemed "a spectral power in thought that walks alone." That power is still alive in the letters we write today. It is within our grasp, and can be felt in the touch of paper and the smell of ink.

There was a time when lives were lived through letters. They spoke to us. Letters were always more than an efficient means of communication: Through them we heard the voices of our friends and loved ones speaking as if they were in the same room with us, sharing our fire, laughing, exchanging news, gossiping—telling us everything. We wrote letters to document, celebrate, and share the most important moments and passages of our lives. In those days, staying in touch meant writing letters. We have many more choices now. Making a phone call and sending E-mail are a lot faster than writing, but despite the conveniences of speed and ease, it is surprising how many of us still love to write and receive letters! Perhaps our appreciation and passion for letters is intensified by the knowledge that no one *has* to write them anymore.

By the time our grandmothers had come of age, the telephone was a relatively new invention that had not yet overtaken the little "duty" notes and bread-and-butter letters that made up the bulk of daily correspondence. The morning and afternoon mails still brought rich caches of elegantly penned requests for weekend visits, invitations to tea and dinner, announcements of train arrivals, and thank-you notes. Indeed, letters of all kinds still flew from house to house, as if to bear witness to the enduring charms of the written word. Personal letters flourished, too, much as they had since the middle of the nineteenth century, when educational reforms gave "ordinary" women more encouragement to read and write. Educated women had long since corresponded and, in some cases, even published collected letters. Madame de Sévigné's, for example, were widely circulated and read in France as early as 1673, while letters written in the last half of the twelfth century by Hildegard of Bingen were read with as much interest during the Crusades as they are today. Long before Jane Austen published her own humorous but highly perceptive novels of middle-class life, Fanny Burney published winning epistolary novels and wrote amusing letters about

Dr. Johnson, who found Mrs. Burney admirable nonetheless. Jane Austen's theory that "the talent of writing agreeable letters is peculiarly female" certainly seems to have been borne out in the decades that followed her death in 1817, for Queen Victoria herself wrote an average of six letters a day, while many of her contemporaries, among them Florence Nightingale and Jane Carlyle, became celebrated for

theirs. What was truly exciting about this fertile letter-writing era was the tremendous flowering of correspondence between women who had none of the advantages of wealth or rank. But thanks to wider literacy and a fast and inexpensive post, women poured their hearts and minds into a veritable snowfall of letters.

For so many of our grandmothers and great-grandmothers, especially those who were separated from family and friends by marriage or distance, letters had become a place, a splendid, intensely personal location where friendships could thrive. Here women could share a remarkable range of experiences and points of view, while being reassured in a wonderfully palpable sort of way that their thoughts and experiences mattered. That someone had taken the time and care to write was in itself a declaration of personal worth. A letter was a vow of friendship.

∽

The Company of Letters

These days we value our friends just as much as our grandmothers did theirs—even if we do write them fewer letters. Perhaps we blame the telephone too much, not to mention the busyness of our lives, for stealing our attention from letter-writing. Ringing phones, busy fax machines, demanding jobs, and the interruptions of children may seem like insuperable obstacles to the peace of mind required for letter-writing, when, in fact, the act of writing itself very often has the effect of slowing down the harried pace of life.

There is something deeply meditative about writing a letter, but sometimes it is difficult to find a pool of calm in which to write one. If we take a few minutes to slow down, breathe deeply, and let our thoughts drift, it doesn't take long to find a still, quiet place inside ourselves. No matter how busy we are, letter-writing gives us time to reflect and slip away from all the noise and clutter in our lives. After spending hours laboring over business letters, Madame de Sévigné found it "relaxing" to write even more! Nothing was more soothing, she said, than to refresh her mind by writing to her daughter. Indeed, mothers seem to have a special knack for stealing letter-writing moments, perhaps because so many of them have had to master the art of improvisation. To catch the mood of the moment or a thought on the fly, Colette's mother would sit at "any old table, pushing aside an invading cat, a basket of plums, a pile of linen, or else just putting a dictionary in her lap by way of a desk."

It seems so much easier to pick up the telephone instead of the pen—even if we have mastered the knack of writing letters under the most adverse conditions—but for most of us there is no real conflict. The telephone is a convenience: It has an immediate use, while letters are timeless repositories of more carefully considered thoughts. Still, good phone calls and good letters share a common ingredient: good conversation. Although the ease and informality of speaking make phone calls seem more immediate, letters can be just as expressive and true. In fact, the more natural a letter sounds, the more we enjoy it. Perhaps the best advice comes from Lord Chesterfield, whose wise and affectionate letters to his son became a famous manual in eighteenth-century England for the moral and social education of young gentlemen. "Write as you speak," he urged. "Write as though you were seated in a room with me, talking in plain, simple language about the things you have seen and done and thought and experienced since you wrote me last." In much the same spirit, James Russell Lowell, a distinguished letter-writer from a century closer to ours, said that letters should "smack a little of the cask"—just like good wine. To leave an imprint of who we are on the letters we write is just as important as it is to speak in our own voice.

At the same time, it is important to take into account the person to whom we are "speaking," just as we would in ordinary conversation. "Draw what all letter-writers instinctively draw," Virginia Woolf advised, "a sketch of the person to whom the letter is addressed. Without someone warm and breathing on the other side of the page, letters are worthless."

Rise of the Spirit of Independence

It always helps to picture the person to whom you are writing and focus your thoughts on how you can give them pleasure. This is surprisingly easy to do in letters to good friends and family, because there is such a deep well of shared experiences to draw from. It is gratifying to know friends so well that we can almost read their minds—and understand instinctively what they like. Just knowing that a letter from us might have the power to delight, amuse, and warm a friend's heart is enough to raise our own spirits.

It is intensely satisfying to be generous with our own sense of pleasure in the letters we write; it makes us feel closer to our friends, as if we'd given them an essential part of ourselves. Letters give us the feeling of being in a friend's presence, sharing their company. When our friends need us, our letters are surely worth more than their weight in gold. Virginia Woolf knew a great deal about the worth of letters, not only the ones she received, but the ones she wrote herself. In his biography of Virginia Woolf, Quentin Bell writes movingly of her epistolary friendship with the painter

Jacques Raverat, who died in the spring of 1925 after a long and painful illness. According to Bell, Virginia Woolf's "instinctive response to suffering was always to write; and her way of showing practical sympathy in illness or distress was to write letters." In a letter to Woolf, just three months before his death, Raverat wrote: "Your letters, particularly the last 3 or 4, have given me something, which very few people have been able to give me in these last years."

Telling the Story of Our Lives

Any good writing—writing that communicates something real and true, including letters to friends—derives its power from our experience of life, whether it's a plain old "day-to-day" life or one fraught with extraordinary events. It doesn't matter. If you tap directly into your own life and allow it to speak for itself, your letters will never fail to be vivid and true.

For many of us the hardest part of writing a letter is getting started—finding the right mood or opening line that will uncork the flow of our thoughts. Sometimes it helps to jump right into a letter, feet first, and start with whatever interesting thought it was that inspired you to write in the first place. Colette did. In a letter to a close friend, she simply dispensed with conventional opening lines: "This morning the sky was a ceiling of airplanes," she wrote.

I know you both better than I did, and love you both better, and always I have a chair for you in the smallest parlor in the world, to wit, my heart. . . .

This world is just a little place, just the red in the sky, before the sun rises, so let us keep fast hold of hands, that when the birds begin, none of us be missing.

Emily Dickinson to her cousins Louise and Frances Norcross, shortly after the death of their mother. The girls had recently visited Dickinson

"How strange it all is, and how eager I am not to die before I have seen it all!" Had Colette resorted to any of the standard openers, such as "How are you?" or "I thought I'd write to say . . . " her letter would have been far less vibrant and her friend wouldn't have felt as if she was right there, standing beside Colette under "a ceiling of airplanes!"

Pulling friends directly into her life through the letters she wrote was Colette's specialty. She had the gift of translating every detail of her life into words that smelled, looked, sounded, and felt exactly like the real thing. In a letter to her friend Jeanne Muhlfeld, Colette paints an intimate and inviting portrait of herself gardening under "a broadrimmed pink calico hat"; wearing "little hobnailed boots"; gorging herself on sun-ripened black cherries; and "turning the color of a pig-skin valise." Charmingly, Colette goes on to describe her account book as "a well-kept flower bed" and apologizes to her friend for not telling her about "the silver dawns and the apricot sunsets" because her mouth is too full of nuts . . .

One of the most inspiring lessons we can learn is that letter-writing truly is organic: Letters are a natural expression of our need to tell the story of our lives. Like Colette, Jane Austen was a habitual letter-writer who poured the events of her life into her novels and letters with equal vigor. She rarely stood on ceremony and entered letters with a brisk, light step. Once, she neatly solved the problem of where to begin a letter to her sister, Cassandra,

Your letter took me quite by surprise this morning. . . . I believe I drank too much wine last night at Hurstbourne. . . . I know not how else to account for the shaking of my hand today; you will kindly make allowance therefore for any indistinctness of writing by attributing it to this venial error. . . .

There were only twelve dances, of which I danced nine, and was merely prevented from dancing the rest by want of a partner. . . . There were very few beauties, and such as there were, were not very handsome. Miss Iremonger did not look well, and Mrs. Blount was the only one much admired. She appeared exactly as she did in September, with the same broad face, diamond bandeau, white shoes, pink husband, and fat neck. . . .

Jane Austen to her sister, Cassandra

by admitting—in the very first line!—that she didn't know: "Where shall I begin? Which of all my important nothings shall I tell you first?"

On another occasion Austen began a letter to Cassandra with the sort of breathless urgency we can only hope to experience from letters: "I have so many little matters to tell you of, that I cannot wait any longer before I begin to put them down." Austen had the courage to say outright—and without embarrassment or polite preamble—that she simply had to write to her sister at that very moment. As for Cassandra, one can only imagine how flattered she must have felt to receive such an urgent, intimate letter.

Talk about not knowing where to begin! On the eve of her marriage, at eighteen, the poet Anne Sexton wrote an excitingly direct letter to her parents. Admirably, the first two lines fly straight to the heart of the matter—but they must have given Anne's parents a terrific jolt: "I don't know how to begin this letter—So I'll jump right in and take my chances. I am eloping with Kayo. By the time you read this you will have another son-in-law."

One of the most comfortable ways to find an opening for your thoughts is to talk about where you are. The beauty of this approach is its simplicity and naturalness, yet it can reveal so much. In a letter to his editor at *The New Yorker*, written from Maine, John Cheever explored an amusing summerhouse phenomenon while expressing a more subtle mood:

Dear Bill,

I wait for this place to unfold. All the summer houses we rent fill up at once with children other than our own. I think it's the groceries. First they creep through the garden and ask if they may use the hammock and the porch furniture. Then they ask for a glass of water (very politely) and settle on the sofa. Then they say that it will be all right with their mothers (who have all gone to Portland) if they remain for lunch. Then they penetrate the bedrooms where they play sardines which is what they are doing now. It is very foggy and to look out of the windows is like looking at a stone. Tuesday was lovely and I have never seen such an evening light anywhere.

As ever,

John

There is certainly nothing prosaic about weather or nature; starting a letter with a description of a seasonal change can spark wonderful observations and reveal an exalted state of mind, as Katherine Mansfield did when she wrote to a friend:

It is such a perfect day—For the last two days and nights I have felt that winter was over for ever and that my breast could not contain my heart. Such air—full of little lilac flowers and new grass and the first butterflies—What can one do with this intolerable love of almost sensa-

*tional life—of the outsides of houses half moonlight and half black
shadow—of the sounds of music and the shapes of people standing in those
round pools of light that the street lamps shed.*

Ultimately, it doesn't matter how you tell the story of your
life, as long as you enjoy telling it. If that pleasure comes through
in the letters you write, you will have succeeded in making people happy, which—as John Cheever put it—is exactly what letters
are supposed to do.

A Voice of Our Own

The secret to writing the kinds of letters people love to read is letting go of preconceived ideas about what a letter should be: what
you can and can't say, and how you should say it. You can be as creative or playful as you like, if it starts the flow of good conversation
on paper. As soon as you give yourself the freedom to write about
anything—in whatever style or voice that suits you—your letters
will be as rich and interesting as you want them to be. Jane Austen,
for example, was once inspired to write to her sister in a mocking,
amused voice, which allowed her to paint a delightfully fanciful, if
somewhat macabre, picture of herself:

You must read your letters over five *times in future before you send them, and then, perhaps you may find them as entertaining as I do. I laughed at several parts of the one which I am now answering.*

You express so little anxiety about my being murdered under Ashe Park Copse by Mrs. Hulbert's servant, that I have a great mind not to tell you whether I was or not.

Emily Dickinson had a wicked sense of humor and loved to lampoon her neighbors just as much as Jane Austen did: "Mrs. Skeeter is very feeble," she wrote to her brother Austin, "can't bear Allopathic treatment, can't have Homeopathic—don't want Hydropathic—Oh what a pickle she is in—shouldn't think she would deign to *live*—it is so decidedly vulgar!" No matter what tone she took in her letters, Dickinson's power to disarm, amuse, and delight was always on display. In a high-spirited letter to old family friends, she points out some of the dubious pleasures of reading the newspaper.

Monday, I solemnly resolved I would be sensible, *so I wore thick shoes, and thought of Dr. Humphrey, and the Moral Law. One glimpse of* The Republican *makes me break things again—I read it every night.*

Who writes those funny accidents, where railroads meet each other unexpectedly, and gentlemen in factories get their heads cut off quite informally? The author, too, relates them in such a sprightly way, that they are quite attractive.

It can be great fun to write a letter in someone else's voice, or from the point of view of a child—or even an animal. John Cheever wrote several letters over the signature of his black Labrador, Cassie, to his good friends the Boyers, who also happened to be the owners of Cassie's mother. This one was addressed to "dear aunt mimi and uncle philip."

Summertime again and dogs writing letters but i thought you'd like to know whether or not i was dead. early on wednesday morning . . . we made a hurried start . . . it was the usual . . . don't put your head out of the window cassie, don't bark at the lady cassie, be a gude dog cassie, etcsteta . . . we had dinner with a very old lady in quincy and then we drove on to wood's hole where pinch-penny shacked the family up in a motel to save a buck.

Writing from Cassie's point of view in his letter to Phil and Mimi Boyer gave John Cheever the freedom to describe his life with bemused detachment and a big dollop of self-irony. It must have been as much fun for him to write this letter as it was for the Boyers to read it.

It becomes easier and feels more natural to write letters once we realize that our lives don't have to be full of earth-shaking moments to be of interest to others. Good friends love to hear about all the various aspects of each other's lives, large and small, from the price of potatoes to the birth of a child to a great sale at Bloomingdale's

I live chiefly on the sofa, but am allowed to walk from one room to the other. I have been out once in a sedan-chair, and am to repeat it, and be promoted to a wheel-chair as the weather serves. On this subject I will only say further that my dearest sister, my tender, watchful, indefatiguable nurse, has not been made ill by her exertions. As to what I owe to her, and to the anxious affection of all my beloved family on this occasion, I can only cry over it, and pray to God to bless them more and more.

Jane Austen to an unnamed correspondent
two months before her death

to an epiphany about the meaning of life. Any detail, no matter how modest, opens up a world of information about the people we love most. Sharing the details of our lives gives us a comforting sense of connection, of being close to each other. In our letters, we can be exactly who we are. In fact, the more we are like ourselves the better. Colette wasn't at all shy about suddenly telling a friend, mid-letter, that she couldn't write any further because she'd eaten some bad mussels. On another occasion, she couldn't help crowing about learning to ski—downhill, no less!—at the tender age of fifty: "I don't miss a chance to fall!" she wrote. In Virginia Woolf's letters, we hear about her affection for sweets, dogs, Spanish wine, and cigars, and learn that she never passed her driver's test—even if she did take lessons; Emily Dickinson gives us the recipe for her prize-winning "rye and indian bread"; and in a delightfully peevish sort of way, Jane Austen owns up to being bored by other people: "Another stupid party last night," she wrote to her sister, Cassandra:

I cannot anyhow continue to find people agreeable; I respect Mrs. Chamberlayne for doing her hair well, but cannot feel a more tender sentiment. Miss Langley is like any other short girl, with a broad nose and wide mouth, fashionable dress and exposed bosom. Admiral Stanhope is a gentlemanlike man, but then his legs are too short, and his tail too long.

Even while Madame de Sévigné was revered by her countrymen as the supreme practitioner of the epistolary art, she chose not to

Dear Friends,
I thought I would write
again. I write you many
letters with pens which
are not seen. Do you
receive them?

Emily Dickinson to Dr. and Mrs. J. G. Hollan

glamorize the events of her life or to disguise her true feelings about them. While taking the curative waters at a fashionable spa in Vichy, she wrote a lively letter to her daughter in which she commented on the celebrated waters ("Ah, how nasty they are!") and described her daily regimen with customary precision and candor:

One goes at six o'clock in the morning to the springs. Everyone is there. One drinks, one makes a terrible face because—just imagine!—the water is boiling hot and has a very strong, very disagreeable taste of saltpeter. One mills around, one comes, one goes, one takes one's promenade, one goes to Mass, one expels the waters and one talks boldly of how one expelled them. That takes up the whole morning. Finally, one dines.

Madame de Sévigné wrote charmingly and at great length about momentous occasions in her life, as well. She was closely associated with the court of Louis XIV, and many of her letters, especially those to her daughter, describe the Sun King's circle in deliciously minute detail. In fact, Madame de Sévigné's letters evoke the era in which she lived with such vividness and accuracy that they are read today in schoolrooms all across France. As indistinguishable as she may be from the important subjects she wrote about, it is the quality of Madame de Sévigné's voice—warm, witty, and intimate—that has captured our hearts, century after century.

When I sit down to write to you, I never think of making any apology, either of haste or any other impediment what-ever. I consider you as a friend, who will take me just as I am, good, or bad, or indifferent.

James Boswell to Sir David Dalrympl

An Unbroken Friendship

No matter how you begin, it always helps to think of a letter as the other half of an ongoing conversation. Sometimes even the most avid writers go through periods where few—if any—letters are exchanged. But it hardly matters: Eventually conversation resumes, as robust and sustaining as it always was.

One of the most appealing aspects of a long–term correspondence is its complete naturalness. Good friends needn't care about propriety or any of the formalities—length, for example. Some of the most personal, and meaningful letters consist of only a few lines. Indeed, lifelong correspondents seem to know instinctively that the best way to keep conversation flowing is to abandon the idea that all letters should be long, soul-searching, or full of exhaustive detail.

Blaise Pascal once quipped that he had written a long letter because he didn't have the time to make it short. For most of us it is the other way around. Just knowing that it's okay to reply to a friend's long letter with a paragraph, or even a single line, can make it easier and much more enjoyable to stay in touch. If you haven't written in a very long while, don't worry about catching up, especially if it means getting bogged down in details. Fire off a short little note instead. It is the spirit of a letter that counts, not the number of pages you've written. Who knows? Maybe you'll be in the mood to write a long, chatty letter next week.

Very often we feel compelled to begin letters—especially the "overdue" ones—with so many apologies that we effectively stop the flow of our own enthusiasm. After heaping on phrases like "I know I should have written sooner," or "I've been meaning to write for a while now, but . . . ," it becomes harder and harder to resuscitate the initial impulse to write. Resist this temptation. Jump right into your letter exactly where you want to start, with whatever interesting thought it was that

inspired you to write in the first place. Don't forget that your friends love you and want to hear from you, no matter what.

A good friend often begins "late" replies to letters with a quick encapsulation of where she is and why she suddenly thought to write. I treasure these letters because they are so spontaneous and affectionate. Each one makes up a link in the unbreakable chain of our friendship:

I'm here. You're there. Are you sitting in the kitchen listening to the kettle boil? I am. My nose is parked right over a big, steaming bowl of tea. The fragrance of lemongrass takes me back to Brooklyn and your yellow kitchen. . . . I'm leaving Moscow for a few days—I need to pry my heat-

damaged brain away from work for awhile. . . . But I'm thinking of you, now that I'm on my way to the country. . . . I know how much you'd love it there . . . the pine scents, the birds, the fresh air. My dacha this year is in Peredelkino, the writers' community, so there's lots of strolling in the evening, and folks stopping in for tea or a drink. Yevtushenko walks his two dogs in the evening: one a ferocious guard dog, the other a magnificent and sweet-tempered white Borzoi named Moroz (Frost). In the twilight (these days around 11 PM), there is nothing more spectacular than seeing ghostlike Moroz loping among the dark pines. . . . I miss you. . . . Write me all about everything.

If you must make an apology for a late reply to a letter, keep Samuel Johnson in mind. Scholars estimate that he wrote well over fifteen hundred letters in his lifetime, not to mention his *Dictionary of the English Language* and *The Lives of the Most Eminent English Poets,* yet Johnson was constantly chided by his friends for not writing sooner or for not writing enough! It is no wonder so many of his letters begin defensively: "I cannot but confess the failures of my correspondence . . . "; "You are not to think yourself forgotten, or criminally neglected, that you have had yet no letter from me . . . ," etc. Yet Johnson's apologies were never stiff or insincere and they certainly did little to stop the Niagaran flow of his words. An apology to his friend Lucy Porter is particularly endearing: "I have not written to you sooner having nothing to say which you would not easily sup-

Do you like the life of yourself? I'm very idle, sitting over the fire; writing with difficulty in a slippery book, while the dog (alas we have two) snore and grumble.
I finished a novel [*To the Lighthouse*]
10 days ago: and already regard it, in which my whole life was wound and boun for 7 months, with complete indifference. I want to buy a motor car, that's all, and wander over the Continent, poking into ruined cities, basking, drinking, writing, like you, in cafés, and talking to Colonels and maiden ladies. Come with me—I will drive: you shall buy grapes and bread, and discuss the state of the wine with natives.

Virginia Woolf to Gerald Brenan

pose, nothing but that I love you, and wish you happy, of which you may be always assured whether I write or not."

The charming but perfectly reasoned defense that Johnson's life was so uneventful that there was nothing to write about actually inspired any number of delightful letters (even if they were a little grumpy) to his good friends Bennet Langton and Joseph Baretti. To Langton he wrote: "You that travel about the world have more materials for letters than I who stay at home, and should therefore write with frequency equal to your opportunities. . . . While you have been riding and running, and seeing the tombs of the learned, and the camps of the valiant, I have only staid at home, and intended to do great things which I have not done. . . . " In his letter to Baretti, he argued rather convincingly that "he who continues the same course of life in the same place, will have little to tell. One week and one year are very like another. . . . I have risen and lain down, talked and mused, while you have roved over a considerable part of Europe; yet I have not envied my Baretti any of his pleasures, though perhaps I have envied others his company." So, apologize if you must, but take inspiration from Dr. Johnson and throw yourself into an utterly charming defense!

It doesn't matter whether we write to friends often or occasionally, briefly or at length, as long as our efforts persist. A letter from a friend is a uniquely lasting form of conversation: It delicately slips through the weave of time, and preserves the moment as completely as a lacewing in a drop of amber.

∞

Only Connect

Abraham Lincoln was an awful speller. Madame de Sévigné rarely used punctuation. Charlotte Brontë's handwriting was so tiny as to be almost invisible, and Katherine Mansfield's was practically illegible. No matter. The main thing about writing letters is to keep writing them. The more you write, the easier it becomes to express yourself. Your friends want to hear from you, even if your letters are not perfectly phrased or studiously grammatical. Don't worry about crossed-out words or a change of ink midstream; the content of your letter is what matters—any little eccentricities of style or presentation will only give it more character. Endless editing and refinement will drain all the freshness and spontaneity from your letter.

There really are no rules about "connecting," even if there are a few considerations to keep in mind. For example, avoid writing at length about people your friend knows nothing about, and it is generally a good idea not to dwell on troubles that seem unresolvable. Still, you should feel free to be as reflective or moody as you like. There's no reason to write a relentlessly cheerful letter if it doesn't reflect your true state of mind; not all letters have to be upbeat.

Write as you feel, but try not to lose sight of the person to whom you are writing.

Even if it's "your turn" to write a letter, wait until you are in the right mood: "I think our best way is just to write to each other whenever we feel an inclination to say something," James Boswell once wrote to his closest friend. "When we are together we never think of parcelling out our sentences in a reciprocal proportion."

And never ever begin or end a letter by telling the person to whom you are writing that you are dashing off your thoughts because you have so many other things to do. On the other end of the letter your friend will read: "Writing to you is less important than a million other things."

If you feel overwhelmed by large, empty sheets of stationery, you can still keep connections alive through a steady flow of short notes and cards. Don't let your fear of writing at length keep you from staying in touch: Write a few lines to a friend on a series of post-cards, or make your own from a recent photograph and jot a message on the back. If the spirit to write moves you while you're on the road, don't wait until you can get your hands on "proper" writing paper—fire off a message on the back of a menu, map, drawing, or photograph. Your friends will be delighted by your spontaneity, not to mention the novelty of the materials you've improvised to stay in touch. This sort of guerrilla correspondence is particularly habit forming because it frees you to communicate in ways that might

Your scrupulous and charming letter has touched me extremely. Dear Rouveyre, you may write me and tell me everything you wish, without wounding or shocking me. Once and for all, I gave you the classification of *friend*. Use it.

Colette to André Rouveyre

feel more natural than the traditional approach to letter-writing.

Keep a supply of interesting cards, photographs, envelopes, pens, notepaper, and stamps on hand. If you do, you'll have everything you need as soon as the mood strikes to write a letter. This wonderful impulse can evaporate very quickly if you have to search interminably for stamps or even a quiet place to

write. As mechanical as it may sound, it really does help to have everything you need for letter-writing in one place.

It is surprising how influential good writing materials can be. Compulsive letter-writers are picky about papers and pens: Colette was passionate about her blue writing paper; Vita Sackville-West was so protective of her big sheets of paper that she locked them up in a special cabinet. Madame de Sévigné also favored large sheets of unlined writing paper, and Virginia Woolf was devoted to her fountain pen, a Penkala, which, she said, wrote all on its own. Sumptuous papers and smooth-nibbed pens, tissue-lined envelopes, and unusual cards are wonderfully staunch letter-writing allies, but the materials themselves needn't be rich or exotic to evoke the best of our friendly thoughts. Whatever comes to hand and feels comfortable is just right.

After all that has been said about the importance of staying in touch and keeping our connections alive, it is easy to forget that

I feel as though I have returned from the seaside with one hot cheek and a feeling of sand between my toes, as I sit down to write to you, my dearest Ottoline. Your wonderful letter which seemed with its spray of verbena to come flying through the gold and green September air dropped in my lap and I read it and sniffed and sniffed the sweet spray and put it at the bottom of a blue jar.

Katherine Mansfield to Ottoline Morrell

something as simple as pleasure is at the bottom of it all. Think of the letters we joyously squirrel away for just the right moment to savor each word, or the letters we ourselves write out of the need to share something essential. These are the letters we delight in most: "I was so pleased and excited by your letter," Virginia Woolf told her sister, "that I trotted about all day like a puppy with a bone." James Boswell wrote to his best friend to tell him that his letters gave him more pleasure than "even glittering guineas do!"; and in a letter to old family friends, Emily Dickinson admitted that she loved to write to them, because it gave her heart "a holiday." What joy there is to be had in friendship. Nothing quite matches it, except, perhaps, the letters we write for our own pleasure and for the enjoyment we hope to bring to someone else.

Ten Special Ways to Stay in Touch

Letters don't always have to be long or serious to count: Some of the most memorable ones we receive—and write ourselves— spring from a natural impulse to share a good joke, a dream, a thought, or a memory. It doesn't really matter what motivates a letter, as long as it keeps friends in touch with each other. It can be as simple and light as a "thank you" for a recipe ("I enjoyed your snap beans in champagne-vinaigrette more than anything else all summer!"); or a poignant way to patch up a quarrel.

A few lines will do, whether you're sending them across town or all the way to Moscow. It is quite fun, not to mention wonderfully liberating, to fire off a snappy, spontaneous little note when there's no particular "reason" to write one:

1. Hide a note in your husband's overcoat—right next to his airplane tickets—before he leaves on a business trip. ("Good luck at the conference. Can't wait till you get back. I love you.")

2. Pop a line or two into your second-grader's lunch box along with an extra-big brownie. ("Here's a special treat for all the time you've been putting into your homework. Good luck on the spelling test—and don't forget how much your mommy loves you, no matter what.")

3. Surprise and touch a close friend, or your own mother or father, with a note saying how much you value their love and friendship. ("Dear Dad, this is just to say how much I love you. I couldn't have gotten through the move to a new house and neighborhood—let alone survived the first year of twins!—without all your encouragement and help. Thank you for everything.")

4. Send a letter to a friend—just to give her the thrill of receiving a personal letter in the mail, instead of the usual bill, advertisement, or catalog.

5. Write a cheery, silly, or affectionate note to a sick child or husband and deliver it on their breakfast tray along with a steaming cup of herbal tea or a special order of pancakes.

6. Send a note to a friend who's in the hospital, just to say "I'm thinking about you," or mail a note to someone you know who needs ongoing encouragement from friends.

7. Tape letters as often as you can to your teenager's bedroom door. ("Hi honey, I'll be here all day Saturday after all. It occurred to me I'd rather spend the day with you—driving to the beach or going to the movies—than sitting around for hours at a boring conference. . . . Let's sleep in.")

8. Delight someone you're getting to know well with a spontaneous note (written on whatever comes to hand—even if it's the back of a menu) that expresses how a perfect sunset, a museum exhibit, or a walk through the woods reminded you of how much you enjoy his or her company.

9. Or, if you're feeling wildly affectionate, send a valentine in the middle of August to anyone you feel passionate about—your husband, best friend, sister, sweetheart, child—or the mysterious new tenant on the fourth floor. . . .

10. Next time you come across an amusing cartoon or photograph in a magazine or newspaper, make a copy and send it to a friend.

Dear Friend,

Everything I am writing is perhaps rather foolish and very presumptuous, beginning with the way I address you, for while I am your friend (though without your willing or knowing it), you are not mine, and then there is something else I must tell you: Until now I have never wished to be another person even for a while, until very recently, when the "Stories of God" came into my hands, and I thought it would be beautiful to have been Ellen Key for a very brief time, so that you would know that I love these stories of God "as no one has before." But seemingly foolish things can be said, after all, and so you will perhaps not laugh at me. I also want so much to tell you what warm gratitude I feel toward you and how much you have given to my music. . . . And so may I thank you, too, good spirit; though words cannot speak from the true fullness of the heart. Perhaps, if life should favor me with the chance of finding you somewhere and sometime in the world, Beethoven's word or a very great one by our Sebastian Bach might say it.—For you love music.

I press your hand!

Magda von Hattingberg to Rainer Maria Rilke

Good Friend,

Let me take up the rich tone of your letter, it becomes my own nature as I read it; what joy that you wrote it, but how good, too, that you weren't able to turn straight away into Ellen Key—that would have complicated matters excessively. Especially since, from the "Stories of God" on, we were both quite dissatisfied with each other's productions. In the end we wrote one another about it with all the loving rudeness that is justified by a long and thoroughly established friendship. . .

. . . Your music lies before me like a season that will eventually come, and if it does not present itself to me here or there, it may happen that I step into its path, the way one goes to Sicily to find the springtime which in the north keeps one waiting and only half hoping. . . .

Farewell, dear friend, or rather, welcome, do not let the new dear fire go out, even though now I will only rarely be able to cast in a small grain of heart resin, to make it fragrant for you.

I am affectionately and gratefully yours.

Rainer Maria Rilke to Magda von Hattingberg

chapter three

Transports of the Heart

Love Letters, Valentines, and Billets-Doux

I wake filled with thoughts of you. Your portrait and the intoxicating evening which we spent yesterday have left my senses in turmoil. Sweet, incomparable Josephine, what is this bizarre effect you have upon my heart!

Napoleon to Josephine

If valentines are the equivalent of a gentle rain, love letters have all the power and unpredictability of a tropical storm. In a state of anticipation that has been likened to a fever—if not madness itself—we wait for love letters, impatiently, hopefully, with cold hands and burning hearts. More than any other form of correspondence, love letters have the power to enslave us and reduce us to something as simple as pure wanting. "All reason is against it," Samuel Butler said, but he would have approved, nonetheless, of a lover such as Julie de Lespinasse, whose passion was searingly artic-ulate: "I have already told you that these words are engraved on my heart, and that they pronounce my doom: to love you, to see you, or to cease to exist."

More than a century after Julie de Lespinasse had given her heart to the indifferent Comte de Guibert, James Joyce wrote a letter to Nora Barnacle that reflected a more contemporary form of roman-tic angst:

It has just struck me. I came in at half past eleven. Since then I have been sitting in an easy chair like a fool. I could do nothing. I hear nothing but your voice. I am like a fool hearing you call me "Dear." I offended two men today by leaving them coolly. I wanted to hear your voice, not theirs.

For some, love is a cataclysm—a disaster on the order of a major flood; or, at the very least, a state of indecision bordering on inertia. For others, love brings mellower weather that lasts well after the first warm days of infatuation. Emily Dickinson would seem to fall into the last category, but it would be wrong to misconstrue her pas-sion as maidenly. Listen to her lovely, full-throated letter to Otis P. Lord and judge for yourself: "I am but a restive sleeper and often should journey from your Arms through the happy night, but you will lift me back, won't you, for only there I ask to be."

Years later, when Dickinson was in her early fifties, the torch she carried for Lord was no less dim: "I am told it is only a pair of Sundays since you went from me," she wrote. "I feel it many years."

∽

Tender Affirmations

Sweet exultation would seem to be the cooler side of love's coin, and, perhaps, it is a more familiar face for those of us who have mined our mothers' and grandmothers' attics for old love letters and antique valentines. Of course, it is always a thrill if something truly torrid turns up, but more often than not the treasures unearthed from scented bureau drawers and musty steamer trunks are gentler proofs of yesterday's love. Still, there is something deeply resonant and wonderfully romantic about the simplest affirmation, whether it was written just last week or fifty years ago, as this one was, by a friend's father:

Darling, As I set out for another week on the road, I think of you and will continue to think of you until my steps bring me home. I'm carrying your little picture with me, the one you gave me last night, when I stood in the doorway for such a long time, finding it impossible to walk away or even move. It will lie close to my heart, darling, and heat my soul, mile after mile, town after town. It's what keeps me going and bears me up.

I have not spent a day without loving you; I have not spent a night without embracing you; I have not so much as drunk a single cup of tea without cursing the pride and ambition which force me to remain separated from the moving spirit of my life. In the midst of my duties, whether I am at the head of my army or inspecting the camps, my beloved Josephine stands alone in my heart, occupies my mind, fills my thoughts.

Napoleon to Josephine

As I got up from my chair, I saw your letter lying on the little round table in front of me. I had to kiss it: then I stood by the fire and looked at the clock and loved you so much that I thought my heart would burst. I wondered whether some thing would tell you that I was full of love of you, wanting you to know I loved you so deeply, at a quarter to twelve on Monday night. Then I got down your photograph. . . . And I was knocked all of a heap by your beauty again. It's the photo where you have the black jacket on, and the marguerite in your button-hole. . . . You darling, darling, darling. . . . You exquisite, incredible woman.

John Middleton Murry to Katherine Mansfield

Once bone white, the paper has since mellowed to the color of butter and feels soft as an old kid glove. One can only imagine how many times this little note has been lovingly handled and read over the years, perhaps during some of the quieter, deeper hours of the night, when it is a comfort to recall a beloved face, a half-forgotten memory, a distant voice.

The Touch of a Love Letter

Philosophers and poets may argue that true love is ephemeral—"a fever of the mind"—or "a mere ghost that everybody talks about but few have seen," as La Rochefoucauld proposed, but lovers know better: It is physical. Love can be made to ring under our feet with all the certainty of stone. Half the joy of receiving a love letter is holding it. Volumes have been written on the nature of love, but nothing is more eloquent than the actual touch and fragrance of a letter as each fold gives up its tender cargo. A love letter is a caress on paper, a kiss that lasts forever.

Letters bring lovers together in a distinctly physical sort of way, which seems to be a heavy component of romance when all is said and done. People who are in love simply want to be near each other, and sometimes a letter is the next best thing. One of the satisfactions of reading other people's love letters is discov-

I suppose animals kept in cages, and so scantily fed as to be always upon the verge of famine, await their food as I awaited a letter. . . . The letter—the well-beloved letter—would not come; and it was all of sweetness in life I had to look for.

Charlotte Brontë

ering how familiar so many of them sound, and how sweetly they express the desire to be close to the ones they love. One might expect a love letter from Henry IV of France, for example, to be cool, regal, and remote, especially if the recipient was the Comtesse de Guiche. Instead he wrote earthily, "How I wish I were in the corner of your fireplace to warm up your soup." This is romance: A king humbling himself in the service of a lady's supper. Henry might not have been there in person, but his letter was, and this extension of himself was no doubt almost as good as the real thing.

Letters have long been loyal ambassadors of the heart, traveling great distances and overcoming every sort of adversity to bring lovers together, even for a momentary embrace. In the heyday of letter-writing, before the ascendancy of the telephone and computer, lovers sometimes commemorated their affections by enclosing fond keepsakes with their letters. A few rose or violet petals might fall from the folds of a young woman's letter or, even better, she might enclose a lock of hair. Photographs were sometimes exchanged, and one can only speculate how dearly these were prized, especially by men and women who were separated by great distances. What power these images, words, and objects must have had to invoke the absent lover's presence.

It might be argued that what we love best about love letters is that they are here at all! How wonderful it is to have tangible proof of love, especially these days when one's beloved is more apt to pick up the telephone than the pen. But even the most ardent telephone conversation eventually fades from memory. A love letter, on the other hand, has undeniable longevity.

Sealed with a Kiss

A letter makes love feel real. Just touching the same paper that has passed through the hands of one's beloved can be intoxicating. Indeed, for those with love in their hearts, the paraphernalia of correspondence has always been heavily invested with romance, from sumptuous writing papers and scented inks to exotic stamps and delicately lined envelopes. All of these elements are carefully considered by the writer, who knows instinctively that the reader will pore over each one with breathless intensity. Love letters, as physical objects, have an almost talismanic power to cast spells and enthrall the mind. Charlotte Brontë gives us a captivating example of this sort of rapture in her novel *Villette* when the narrator, Lucy Snowe, receives a letter from the man she loves:

Having feasted my eyes with one more look, and approached the seal, with a mixture of awe and shame and delight, to my lips—I folded the untasted treasure, yet all fair and inviolate, in silver paper, committed it to the case, shut up box and drawer, reclosed, relocked the dormitory and returned to class, feeling as if fairy tales were true and fairy gifts no dream. Strange, sweet insanity! And this letter, the source of my joy, I had not yet read: did not yet know the number of its lines.

"Strange sweet insanity" perfectly describes the white-hot state of anticipation in which we sometimes find ourselves—if we are lucky—but quieter moods can inspire love letters, too. Katherine Mansfield once closed a letter to her husband with a lyrical evocation of love:

I love you tonight beyond measure. Have I ever told you how I love your shoulders? When I hold you by your shoulders—put my arm round you & feel your fine delicious skin—warm & yet cool, like milk—and your slender bones—the bones of your shoulders . . .

There's an incantatory sound to Mansfield's voice—an obvious delight in "counting the ways." A love letter is a good place to record the progress of the heart, even if the message never varies. Regardless of style, the same three little words—*I, love, you*—continue to persist, unchanged. They poke up through the lines and spaces of every love letter with all the tenacity of a healthy weed.

It is the hardest thing in the world to be in love and yet attend to business. As for me, all who speak to me find me out, and I must lock myself up or other people will do it for me.

A gentleman asked me this morning, "What news from Lisbon?" and I answered, "She is exquisitely handsome." Another desired to know when I had been last at Hampton Court. I replied, "It will be on Tuesday come se'nnight. Prythee, allow me at least to kiss your hand before that day, that my mind may be in some composure." O love!—

A thousand torments dwell about me! Yet who would live to live without thee?

Methinks I could write a volume to you; but all the language on earth would fail in saying how much and with what disinterested passion I am ever yours.

Sir Richard Steele to Mary Scurlock

An Enduring Love

Now that people can make connections instantaneously through E-mail or over the telephone, one might wonder if there is any use at all for love letters. Do people still write them? The answer is, emphatically, yes! Indeed, love letters demand to be written and answered. Nothing makes us feel as exalted or, at the same time, more vulnerable than love; once it has inspired us to spill our hearts on paper, we yearn for a confirming echo of our own fervor. Of course, one can coo happily over the telephone for hours on end, or print amorous E-mail, but it's just not quite the same as receiving a love letter through the mail. For one thing, part of the joy of receiving a love letter, though it sounds perverse, is surviving the long and anguished wait for it. The post office itself confers a certain mystery on love letters, as it does on almost every other aspect of its operations. After you've written a letter and dropped it into a mailbox, the sense of having committed your affections to a black hole becomes all too pungent. Will the letter ever make its way to its destination? And if so, when? Phone calls are rarely this suspenseful, and E-mail can't possibly deliver the sort of drama that letter-carriers provide. Even the envelope of a love letter—emblazoned with a familiar hand—has the power to transport our senses.

Although it is true that technology now allows us to communicate with terrific speed and convenience, one can't help wondering if the

While I was writing the last page, tear after tear fell on the paper. But I must cheer up—Catch!—An astonishing number of kisses are flying about . . . I see a whole crowd of them! Ha! Ha! . . . I have just caught three—They are delicious!

Wolfgang Amadeus Mozart to his wife, Constanze

human heart has evolved quite as quickly as the microchip. With all the emphasis we've placed on making our connections happen faster and faster, have we really gotten any better at staying in touch? Perhaps the heart's greatest charm (even if it is a little politically incorrect) is its willingness to squander our most precious commodity: time. A love letter allows us to escape the tyranny of the clock; it has the power to make time stand still, and gives us permission to wallow and luxuriate for as long as we like in the warm bath of another's affection. There's never any hurry.

We are still remarkably tactile creatures, despite all our refinements, and letters help satisfy a basic need to touch and hold the people we love most. There is simply nothing more personal than a love letter. If the ones we've had the courage to send are outright declarations of love, then the ones we receive in return prove that our own feelings have been taken seriously. This sort of acknowledgment is priceless.

⌒

The Luxury of Letting Go

With so much invested in a love letter, one might quake before the proposition of actually writing one, but there is nothing to fear. If anything, love letters fall into the range of "rogue correspondence," where there are no rules to follow and the heart is free to blaze a

How happy your last letters have made me—those since Christmas Eve! I should like to call you by all the endearing epithets, and yet I can find no lovelier word than the simple word "dear," but there is a particular way of saying it. My dear one, then, I have wept for joy to think that you are mine, and often wonder if I deserve you. . . . But how light-hearted I was yesterday and the day before! There shone out of your letters so noble a spirit, such faith, such a wealth of love! What would I not do for love of you, my own Clara! The knights of old were better off; they could go through fire or slay dragons to win their ladies, but we of today have to content ourselves with more prosaic methods, such as smoking fewer cigars, and the like. After all though, we can love, knights or no knights; and so, as ever, only the times change, not men's hearts.

Robert Schumann to Clara Schumann

path of its own. Maybe Jean-Jacques Rousseau was right when he suggested that love letters should "begin without knowing what we intend to say, and end without knowing what we have written."

Just like any other form of personal correspondence, love letters boil down to pure self-expression: You can be as extravagant, elegant, witty, poetic, passionate, saucy, silly, or simple as your heart desires. What could possibly be more enjoyable or give you greater freedom to be yourself? The trick is to abandon any pretense of invulnerability. The best thing to do, once you've been struck, is to succumb utterly and give free rein to your most amorous impulses. Don't worry for a minute about sounding sappy; and remember that nothing is more absurd than a well-balanced love letter. In fact, the object of your affections will be immensely flattered by the devastating effect he or she has had on your ability to think clearly or behave rationally. Just say what you really feel.

There's only one caveat to keep in mind: No matter how extravagantly you express yourself, don't forget that sincerity is the most important ingredient in a love letter. Without it, your claim to another's heart is worthless. But for those who are genuinely smitten, sincerity is rarely an issue. You simply can't go wrong if you stay true to the real goal of a love letter, which is, after all, to bring encouragement and joy to someone you love.

chapter four

Please Join Us

A Word About Etiquette

Not so long ago, most of our social correspondence was made up of
"letters of etiquette," the little notes one was obliged to write on
special occasions. These included thank-you notes, invitations, and
notes of congratulation and condolence.

As improbable as it may seem to those of us who now communicate
with each other almost exclusively over the telephone or by electronic
mail, these so-called "duty" letters once ruled and mediated our
social lives. But being subject to them wasn't all drudgery. There was a
good deal of comfort to be had, not to mention convenience, in knowing the prescribed forms of social communication. One rarely
felt at sea, or at a loss for words—even in response to the most difficult
circumstances—if one was well-schooled in the correct forms of
correspondence. Eventually, with so much use, the forms became
automatic and, at the same time, less static. Skilled practitioners em-
bellished, enlivened, and generally enjoyed writing even the most basic
forms of correspondence. Self-irony and humor were not rare commodi-
ties and were often gloriously represented in daily correspondence.

What has not vanished with our grandmothers' crinolines and

hooped skirts is etiquette, although it may sound as old-fashioned. Perhaps a better word for etiquette is respect—that elusive but essential quality we prize so highly in our relationships. At the same time, etiquette is a wonderfully convenient "social unguent"; as a good friend wisely defines it: Etiquette keeps our social lives running smoothly.

Even now many of the old "rules" are very much alive in our correspondence, not because they are required or expected, but because they make such good sense. Knowing them, you can write the occasional "bread and butter" note for an enjoyable weekend; a thank-you note for an unexpected gift; a note of congratulation on the birth of a child; or you can accept an invitation to a moonlight picnic or a formal wedding with equal confidence and zest.

The main thing to remember about social correspondence is that it has a purpose and a specific job to do. In other words, the main thrust of an invitation should be information: the date, time, and place of an occasion; while the focus of a condolence letter should be on the thoughts and feelings of the bereaved, rather than on oneself. Our personal correspondence, on the other hand, may be as digressive and ample as we like.

The importance of the most informal, brief, or simple social communication should be reflected in the quality of the materials used to convey the message, the subtext of which always is: "You are valued."

Although many people now type most of their correspondence, it is generally accepted that the more gracious and personal gesture is to write by hand all notes of invitation, thanks, and, especially, condolence. It is also proper etiquette, that is to say, it is a genuine sign of respect, to send a note of sympathy or appreciation as quickly as possible. A prompt response is a sign of vigorous and authentic concern; nothing could be more flattering or touching to the recipient.

Writing and responding to formal correspondence (such as an invitation to a traditional wedding or a ceremonial dinner) is much less difficult than it sounds because it relies on formula, instead of originality—which is much less predictable. A response to a formal invitation actually involves less writing than the simplest note of informal reply. The rules are so straightforward that you simply can't go wrong. The main thing to remember about any formal communication is to respond *in kind*. A reply to a formal invitation, for example, should mirror the exact style of the invitation: If it is written by hand in the third person, the reply should also be written by hand in the third person. Simply use the invitation as a model, and write on plain, good-quality note or letter paper.

In the final wash, it doesn't really seem to matter how doggedly we follow rules or traditions, as long as the important connections we yearn to make with each other are made. To do so with kindness and wisdom, wit and practicality, may require a small investment of time and effort, but it is well worth making.

Invitations and Announcements

Come and have tea tomorrow evening with my wife and me. I will ask the young man to come. You probably know his name: it is Pierre Curie.

Marie Sklodowska was a twenty-seven-year-old science student and researcher living in Paris, when she received this invitation from Polish friends. She accepted, and what began with a simple cup of tea resulted in courtship, marriage, and an enduring scientific partnership with Pierre Curie.

Not all invitations are destined to spark lasting friendships or powerful unions, but each one, no matter how informal, contains a grain of that promise. At the very least, an invitation provides an opportunity to widen the circle of friends around us.

Invitations carry our hearts across oceans and continents—or just across town—to summon family and friends to share the joy of weddings and birthdays, graduations and parties. These special occasions give us a chance to renew our most cherished ties and rekindle those that may have lapsed over the years. What better time is there to make use of our most elegant stationery, loveliest cards, rarest inks, and finest sentiments?

Although most invitations these days are much less formal than they once were, there are occasions where a little knowledge of invitation etiquette comes in handy. Years ago, politely worded invitations to tea, dinner, parties, balls, weddings, bridal showers, and weekend visits were invariably handwritten and, quite often, delivered by hand. Life was a more formal affair altogether, so much so that it was considered proper for a gentleman to invite a young lady—in writing—if he wished to ride with her for as little as an hour or two. Such an invitation might read:

Mr. Waterbury presents his compliments to Miss Dawson, and would be much pleased if she will accompany him in a drive to Pine Hills, this afternoon at 4 o'clock.

To which the young lady might reply:

Miss Dawson's compliments to Mr. Waterbury; she accepts with pleasure his kind invitation for this afternoon.

An answer declining the gentleman's invitation would be just as cordial:

Miss Dawson regrets that an important engagement will prevent her accepting Mr. Waterbury's kind invitation for this afternoon.

Using the third person to refer to oneself is a formal convention that survives to this day, although it is used only on very formal occasions, such as a traditional wedding or a "white-tie" dinner.

There aren't many hard-and-fast rules about invitations now, and what few remain can be easily mastered. Most of the "rules" boil down to common sense and good old-fashioned consideration for other people. In the end, the important thing is to make a connection.

Invitations are a particularly gracious form of connection and call for respectful handling. When sending an invitation, be sure to include all of the pertinent information about the occasion, place, date, and time. This will save guests the embarrassment of arriving late, or on the wrong day. Remember that all the care given to detail in an invitation is a reflection of the host's esteem for the guest. There fore, a quick and gracious reply is an echoing statement of the guest's esteem for the host. Mutual respect is the core of etiquette. In that spirit, always be definite about accepting or declining an invitation. If you leave your host in doubt by suggesting, for example, that you will attend her wedding and reception only if you are able to return from an overseas business trip on time, she will not know for sure whether or not to plan on your attendance. This kind of uncertainty creates tension and inconvenience for a host, especially if food preparation, special seating, or overnight accommodations are involved.

If circumstances are such that you must turn down an invitation, a swift reply is always appreciated. When there is simply not enough time to reply in writing, a telephone call or E-mail is exactly the right way to respond. However, if you have time to send a short, handwritten note by "snail mail," the host will be flattered and immensely pleased that you took the time to write.

Although it is customary to keep invitations and their replies short and to the point, there are circumstances when the rules—relaxed as they are—can be bent even more. In declining an invitation, especially from a good friend, one can indulge in a little self-mockery or, perhaps, a strong dose of whimsy. For the reclusive poet Emily Dickinson, an invitation for a weekend visit elicited just such a response:

My dear Abiah, my warmest thanks are yours, but don't expect me. I'm so old fashioned, Darling, that all your friends would stare. I should have to bring my work bag, and my big spectacles, and I half forgot my grandchildren, my pin-cushion, and Puss.

Writing to each other allows us to share something of our deeper selves, even when declining special invitations. The French writer Colette was profoundly moved by her mother's reason for declining a visit:

My pink cactus is probably going to flower. It is a very rare plant I've been given, and I'm told that in our climate it flowers only once every four years. Now, I am already a very old woman, and if I went away when my pink cactus is about to flower, I am certain I shouldn't see it flower again.

Virginia Woolf, who was as avid a correspondent as Colette, wrote as many as six letters a day and sent many dozens of invitations to tea, dinner, and weekend visits. "Life would split asunder without letters," she once wrote. The same could be said of written invitations. Woolf's were usually brief and very often amusing. In a note to her friend and brother-in-law Clive Bell, she explained why she had written to invite him to tea, rather than use the telephone: "I can't face your blasted telephone, which kicks in my ear like an infuriated mule."

There *is* something to writing a little note of invitation, rather than face the collective assault of answering machines, perpetually busy phone lines, or even a ring as offensive as Clive Bell's. Still, it is pointless to deny the speed and convenience of the telephone and electronic mail, especially when so many people are using one or the other—if not both—for their regular correspondence. Indeed, it is perfectly acceptable now to use the telephone or E-mail to invite people to just about any sort of casual get-together, from lunch, brunch, tea, drinks, and dinner, to picnics, parties, barbecues, dances, and weekends away. For more formal occasions, however, it is still customary to send a personal, handwritten card or a note. If inspiration fails, or, as is more often the case, there simply isn't enough time to write personal notes, never fear: There are excellent alternatives.

Most stationers', gift, and card shops offer a huge selection of commercial preprinted or fill-in invitations that can be used for almost any occasion or milestone. Handmade invitations are becoming more popular, but if you opt to make one, be sure that all the important information—place, date, time, and directions—is legible. It is also a courtesy to let your guests know ahead of time what they might expect. For example, it is always helpful to know how formal or informal an occasion will be, and whether or not anything out of the ordinary should be brought, such as beachwear for an outdoor party or a covered dish for a potluck. If your guests have all the information they need before arriving, they will be prepared to enjoy themselves thoroughly and without misgiving.

Now that most social events are relatively casual, one really doesn't need to be overly concerned with prescribed forms. However, there are a few occasions, such as traditional weddings and "sit-down" dinners, that require a little familiarity with customary protocols. Under these circumstances, it is best to consult a good stationer or one of the many excellent etiquette books that describe exactly how to write and respond to formal wedding invitations.

If you are planning an informal wedding, however, and wish to write a more personal or unusual invitation, there are many ways to do so. Indeed, these invitations may be as individual as the people who send them: There was a delightful piece in *The New York Times* recently about a couple who printed their invitations "on yellowed pieces of paper, burnt around the edges like a pirate's treasure map, and rolled up inside clear plastic bottles with sand, tiny shells and bits of dune grass. The labels had pictures of a full moon at the beach, with the addresses typed over the surf." It must have been refreshing to receive such a creative invitation, but a simple handwritten note can be just as memorable.

Informal Wedding Invitations

Most informal wedding invitations are written by hand on plain, good-quality card or note paper. Double sheets, like those used for engraved invitations, are still used to lend a touch of elegance to an informal wedding. If a small wedding is planned, the bride's mother sometimes writes a few invitations herself, either to special friends of the marrying couple or a close friend of her own. Most women are so busy these days that preprinted and fill-in cards have become a popular alternative to handwritten notes. However, if you do have a little extra time, informal wedding invitations can provide marvelous opportunities for self-expression. The note-in-a-bottle invitation described above was perfect for a relaxed and joyful wedding on the beach, and what could be more romantic or personal?

If you choose to design your own wedding invitations, please be sure that all the information—date, place, and time—is legible. It is also very helpful to enclose a map or directions to the wedding, if they are needed.

Invitations to an informal wedding may be mailed as late as ten days before the wedding, although it is always a courtesy to give guests as much time as possible to plan for the occasion.

To a relative

Dear Aunt Rebecca,

Paul and I have planned a simple wedding for Sunday, the third of October, at three o'clock, in the little chapel at St. Mark's. Nothing would make us happier than to see you there, with us, when we get married.

Would you join us after the ceremony for a small reception at the Ocean Club?

Paul sends his love, and we both have the highest hopes that you will join us on the third.

Love,

Diana

To a friend

Dear Elizabeth,

You are the very first to hear our news, which I was tempted to tell you over the phone, but I wanted to be sure you were sitting down when you heard it. John and I have decided to get married. Next month! At my parents' house on Cape Cod. The wedding will be at six o'clock on Saturday, July 15th, unless one of us runs away first. Afterward, our old friends Edward and Marie Snowe will host a reception for all of us at their cottage, two doors down. Are you free to ride up to the Cape with us after work on Thursday, the thirteenth? John promises not to drive the way he usually does. We are also hoping you'll agree to stay in your old room at Mom and Dad's (nothing has changed—not even the awful bed with the dip in the middle). Please say you'll come anyway. John and I couldn't face the prospect of finally saying "I do" without you.

Love,

Jenny

To special friends, from the bride's mother

Dear Mr. and Mrs. Freund,

We are hoping you will give us the great pleasure of your presence at Kate and Ted's wedding on March twenty-seventh at four o'clock. The ceremony and the reception will be held at our apartment. We would be delighted if you joined us in celebrating this happy occasion. Ted and Kate have often spoken of you with so much affection that we are especially eager to meet you, and to share their special day with you.

Sincerely,

Lydia Holt

Ingrid Smollet and Peter Jones
invite you to celebrate their marriage on
Saturday, September the sixth
at four o'clock
The Boat House
Prospect Park, Brooklyn

Replies to an Informal Wedding Invitation

Replies to informal wedding invitations should be made promptly, no matter how well one knows the bride or groom. Even for a casual wedding, plans require plenty of lead time, so it is a courtesy to let the bride know as soon as possible whether or not you can attend. Although friends and family may telephone to accept or decline the invitation, it is always a good idea to answer with a little note, as phone messages can get lost or misplaced. A personal note is also a thoughtful way to celebrate a close friend's marriage. A simple note of congratulation may be written on personal stationery or any good-quality card or notepaper.

Relative's acceptance

Dear Diana,

What a lovely invitation. Yes, I'd love to come to your wedding and reception on October third. I'm so pleased! The first time I met Paul, at that wonderful picnic in Central Park last spring, I knew he was someone very special.

Please give my love to your parents, and to Paul. I can't tell you how much I'm looking forward to seeing all of you at the wedding.

Lovingly,
Aunt Rebecca

Friend's acceptance

Dear Lucy,

Of course I'll come to your wedding. I can't imagine being anywhere else. It was awfully nice of your folks to invite me to stay at the house, and I don't really mind at all about the dippy mattress in the guestroom. I just hope your parents are prepared to keep me around for the next twenty years. I can hardly wait to trap you in the back seat and get a chance to get the scoop on everything. Mostly, though, I'm looking forward to seeing my best friend get married to the nicest man I think I've ever met.

Love,

Elizabeth

Friend's regret

Dear Jenny,

I'm so sorry I won't be able to be with you and John on the fifteenth of July. I would love to have seen you get married, especially since I like to think I was the first person to introduce you to John. Now look what's happened.

The baby's due date has been pushed up a week, and it probably makes more sense to stay close to home than go where my fondest thoughts will surely be on the fifteenth.

Charles and I wish you and John all the best, and hope to see you very soon after the wedding. We're keeping something very French, very expensive, and very bubbly on ice—just for you.

Love,

Louisa

Bridal and Baby Showers

In lieu of a commercial fill-in invitation, or an engraved or printed card, one may send an informal note or short letter of invitation, such as the one on the next page, to a bridal or baby shower. Personal stationery or a plain, good-quality card may be used.

If guests are asked to bring a particular kind of gift, such as lingerie or housewares, to a bridal shower, the invitation should state the bride's sizes and color preferences. Bridal showers are generally held from two weeks to two months before the wedding.

A baby shower for an expectant mother can be given at almost any time, although it is probaby wise to schedule the shower at least one month to six weeks before the baby's due date.

A baby shower for a new mother should be given once she has had all the time she needs to adjust to her baby's schedule and feels completely comfortable about receiving visitors.

Replies to shower invitations may certainly be made over the telephone, but it is a lovely gesture to return the favor with a short note.

Invitation

Dear Paula,

I'm sure you must remember our plans to arrange a surprise shower for Nora, even if some of the details did get thrown out with our cocktail napkins at Nick's Lounge the other night. Never fear, I remember everything—even your mother's recipe for Brunswick stew—which I propose to serve at the shower, at my house, on Saturday, January the fifteenth. How does one o'clock sound?

I think your idea of showering Nora with wonderful things for the house is excellent. She and Gabe will need just about everything when they move in together this spring. Of course, I can hardly wait to see you on the fifteenth.

Yours,

Susan

Friend's acceptance

Dear Susan,

It will be a great pleasure to come to Nora's shower on the fifteenth. I'm really looking forward to seeing how surprised Nora will be when she sees all of us! Please give me a call if there's anything I can do to help out. . . . It is not beneath me to peel potatoes or wash pans, by the way. I entertain rather nicely, too, as you might recall from my performance a while back at Nick's Lounge.

Sincerely,

Paula

Friend's regret

Dear Susan,

Thank you so much for inviting me to Nora's shower on January fifteenth, but I am sorry I won't be able to come. Ron and I will be in Boston that weekend for his nephew's Bar Mitzvah. May I send a gift for Nora to your house? I found something I think she'll really like, and would be so pleased if you could give it to her with my love. My thoughts will be with her—and with all of you on the fifteenth.

Sincerely,

Joanna

∞

Informal Dinner

The details of a dinner invitation given over the telephone may be forgotten. A note reminds guests of the occasion and saves them the embarrassment of calling if they have forgotten where, or at what time, they are expected.

Invitation

Dear Fiona,

Lewis and I would be so pleased if you and Tom could join us for dinner on Friday, March the eleventh, at seven o'clock. Too much time has passed since we last saw you, and we are eager to hear all your news, especially about the trip to Indonesia.

Most sincerely,

Lenore Campbell

Acceptance

Dear Mrs. Campbell,

Tom and I were so happy to receive your kind invitation to dinner on March eleventh, at seven o'clock.

It's true, too much time has gone by since we last saw you. We look forward with great pleasure to spending an evening with you and Mr. Campbell. Be forewarned, though, Tom is bringing three shoe boxes (size 13½!) full of photographs from the trip.

Sincerely yours,

Fiona Tate

Regret

Dear Mrs. Campbell,

Tom and I were so happy to receive your kind invitation to dinner on March eleventh, but I'm afraid we won't be able to come. Both of us will be at a trade show in Atlanta through the night of the fifteenth. We would love to get together

with you and Mr. Campbell, though, sometime soon. We miss you both, and are
very eager to show you all the wonderful photos we took on the trip.

Sincerely yours,
Fiona Tate

Informal Wedding Announcements

An informal announcement can be just as beautiful and express as much dignity as a more formal one. It can combine traditional language with unusual materials or it can follow your own wording on

customary materials (plain, good-quality note, card, or letter paper). But there is lots of room for originality. Almost any style or design is acceptable as long as it expresses the spirit of the occasion.

Informal announcements may be sent at almost any time, although most people mail them just before or directly after the wedding.

No reply is required. Good friends, business associates, or clients may, of course, respond with a note or letter of congratulation. Sending an announcement is just another good way to narrow the distance between friends or family who may live far away, but who would, undoubtedly, be happy to hear the good news. Indeed, the receipt of an announcement might initiate more correspondence.

From the parents of the bride and groom

....

Share with us our joy in announcing

the marriage of our daughter

Ingrid to

Mr. Justin St. Cloud

on Sunday, the first of May

at half after seven o'clock in the evening

at Church of the Holy Cross

New Haven, Connecticut

....

From the bride and the groom

....

Ingrid Smollet and Peter Jones

are happy to announce the celebration

of their marriage

on Saturday, September the sixth,

at four o'clock

The Boat House, Prospect Park, Brooklyn

....

Birth Announcement

Although store-bought fill-in cards are now generally used to announce the birth or adoption of a baby or child, some families design their own cards or send a more formal engraved or printed announcement. No matter how formal or informal the card may be, the message is invariably one of the happiest ones ever sent to family and friends. Enjoy this opportunity to spread the wonderful news.

....

Mr. and Mrs. Roger Cohen have the happiness
to announce the birth of a daughter, Nina,
on Monday, March the twenty-fifth,
nineteen hundred and ninety-eight

....

For a child, or children, adopted by a couple

....

Paul Wells and Maryanne Richards
are proud and happy
to announce the adoption of
Oona Wells-Richards
born April 2, 1997, arrived from
Hunan Province, China, November 27, 1998

....

Post Ca

THIS

chapter five

The Words to Say It

Thank-You Notes and
Letters of Congratulation

Since I have no sweet flower to send you, I enclose my heart; a little one, sunburnt, half broken sometimes, yet close as the spaniel, to its friends.

Emily Dickinson, for a gift of flowers

Thank-You Notes

Of all the letters and notes we write, thank-you notes are usually the most enjoyable. For some of us, however, the tricky part is writing them before too much time has gone by; the longer we wait to write them, the more difficult it becomes to express our thanks with freshness and sincerity. It is much easier and a lot more fun to write these little notes if you approach them as you would anything else that gives you pleasure. As soon as you receive a gift, take a few minutes to express your thanks spontaneously, while the glow of enthusiasm is still strong. Thank-you notes are meant to be short, so there's no need to spend too much time writing them. Enjoy yourself while you write. If that pleasure comes through in your note, the person who receives it will feel happy, too.

It is gracious to acknowledge every gift or act of kindness, and every expression of hospitality—no matter how small—with a thank-you note. Even if it is quite short, a thank-you note still has the power to convey and preserve your friendly thoughts long after a conversation or phone call has faded from memory.

Ideally, one shouldn't feel obliged to write a thank-you note, particularly if one's heart isn't in it, but there are circumstances that make it advisable nonetheless. For example, even if you know that you will never wear the scratchy woolen scarf your great-aunt Elizabeth knitted for your birthday, the right thing to do is to send a note of thanks anyway. Undoubtedly, there will be many other opportunities to acknowledge gifts with complete sincerity; in the meantime, it is an act of grace and generosity to acknowledge the thoughtfulness of another, even if it has misfired a bit. The last thing you'd want is your great-aunt to feel disappointed by a note that was written out of duty instead of affection.

Thank-you notes have no particular formula. However, there are a few simple ways to give them interest and vitality. For example, instead of saying "Thank you for the flowers," you can express your gratitude in a more specific way, as Colette once did: "The daphnes have arrived, fresh and intact, and their fruity odor fills the room where I am writing."

A little humor or a touch of self-revelation can also give a simple note the weight of a more personal letter: "My dear Gerald," Virginia Woolf once wrote, "I think I appreciate lilies more than the altars do—nevertheless, I don't approve of this lavish generosity of yours. Do I send you venison if you have a cold? At the same time, your lilies are triumphant and resplendent in my big jar. Thank you very much."

There are a surprising number of occasions that provide opportunities to say thank you, not only for gifts, but for special favors and acts of kindness as well.

Less than two months before she died, Jane Austen wrote to her nephew to thank him for an intangible gift that meant the world to her:

I know no better way my dearest Edward, of thanking you for your affectionate concern for me during my illness, than by telling you myself as soon as possible that I continue to get better. . . . God bless you my dear Edward. If ever you are ill, may you be as tenderly nursed as I have been.

Acknowledgment of a favor—that might have had less significance under normal circumstances—took on extra meaning and immediacy when it was communicated to Renée Hamon in a note by the inexhaustible Colette. It was written from Paris in the cold, hungry winter of 1940, when the city was under siege by Germany. But in mid-December, Renée Hamon worked a miracle; she smuggled a box of food into Paris. Colette's thank-you was as vibrant and ferociously tender as the writer herself:

Quick, quick, a line to praise the beautiful package! I'll write presently at length, but let me just acknowledge that everything has arrived. The pink potatoes, and above all the GARLIC! Here it is absolutely not to be found. Two francs for half a clove, and even so it's not to be had. So you'll realize what a treasure trove you have sent me. And the reddish-brown onions! And the princely apples! You are a love of a little pirate—and to cap it all, the herbs!

The things for which we are thankful may seem mundane after we've read Jane Austen's or Colette's letters, but in all likelihood they would disagree: It's the spirit that counts. So, when writing a thank-you note for a gift received on a birthday, holiday, graduation, or wedding, the key is to remember how happy you felt, and to write about that happiness with honesty and enthusiasm—in your own voice.

∞

For Wedding Gifts

Almost as soon as wedding invitations are mailed, gifts start pouring in (or at least we wish they did). Virginia Woolf found the occasion daunting and yet so delightful that she wrote an amused note to her good friend Violet Dickinson: "When will the presents cease? What other operation of nature can you provide for? Anyhow, we shall drink out of your glasses to the end of our lives, so long as we have a table to stand them on. They are perfect."

If you have the good fortune to be overwhelmed by a landslide of wonderful gifts, you can easily avoid the embarrassment of either forgetting who sent a particular gift—or thanking someone for a gift they didn't send—if you keep a record of gifts and their senders' addresses in one place (a small notebook, for example).

Most people do not expect a thank-you note immediately after they've sent a wedding gift: Working couples rarely have time to send notes before returning to full-time jobs. Once the dust has settled, however, it is usually the bride who writes the thank-you notes, unless she has managed to send them out before the wedding, which is customary, or during the honeymoon, which is also customary, but not very likely these days. In any case, it is acceptable for the bride to write thank-you notes after the honeymoon, and to involve her husband in the process, if he chooses to help. In earlier days, the wife was expected to write all thank-you notes, including those to her husband's friends and business associates, even if she didn't know them or had never seen them before.

Although a variety of preprinted thank-you cards are available at stationery and gift shops, it is still a gracious gesture to handwrite all thank-you notes, even those to clients and business associates. This can be done on plain, good-quality notepaper or stationery.

Even if you have received dozens of wedding gifts, the time spent writing thank-you notes is well worth the effort. It doesn't matter if your notes are short: The people who receive them will be pleased and flattered that you took the time to thank them in such a personal way.

It is very gratifying to the recipient of a thank-you note to know what you like, specifically, about their gift. For example, instead of saying, "Thank you so much for the present," you might say that "the beautifully framed botanical prints" you were given "perfectly match the decor" of your study; or that a gift of china is "the ideal complement to a set of dishes" you already have (and which you adore). People love to be told how wisely they've chosen a gift; your appreciation of their choice will deepen their pleasure in having made you happy.

Dear Nora,

Now that you've sent us such exquisite china, Ned and I will have to flee our miserable digs and move to a much more refined environment, say, Buck-

ingham Palace? At least we can offer the Queen coffee in cups more beauti-
ful than anything the Royal kitchens might send up.

The best way we can offer our thanks, Nora, for the beautiful coffee ser-
vice is to exact a promise from you that you'll visit us here (not at the
Palace), as soon as possible. We want to shower you with all our affection—
not to mention Ned's prized Jamaican Blue Mountain coffee, which I will
bring to you every morning on a tray, in the prettiest cup in the world.

Love,

Antonia

Dear Uncle Robert and Aunt Victoria,

An ordinary "thank you" seems woefully inadequate as an acknowledgment
of your incredible wedding present to John and me. The check you sent made
our heads spin. If you only knew how much it means to us, you would be
very happy, as I'm sure you must be, knowing that thanks to you, we will
be able to travel on our honeymoon.

John and I are now pawing happily and frantically through glossy
brochures—just like the proverbial kids in a candy store—searching for the
perfect Caribbean getaway. Thank you from the bottom of our hearts for giv-
ing us this rare and fantastic treat. Your kindness and generosity has made
all the difference for John and me, as we begin our life together.

All my love,

Jenny

∽

For a Bridal Shower

Even if you have already thanked friends in person for their gifts, it is always a welcomed courtesy to follow up with a note of thanks.

Dear Thea,

I'm still not over the delightful thrill of the surprise shower. I don't think I'll ever forget how completely surprised I was when you opened the door; I had never seen so many familiar faces in one place before! Thank you for orchestrating such a wonderful party.

Pat and I are overwhelmed by the beautiful bed and bath things we received from all of you. Your duvet cover is particularly splendid. . . . And it goes with all my new bed linens. Thanks again, Thea, for hosting the shower. It couldn't have been more perfect. I will always remember it as one of the happiest days of my life.

With love,
Rachel

∽

For a Baby Shower and Newborn Gifts

Most people absolutely love to buy baby things for their friends because it is so much fun: The impossibly tiny socks, dresses, T-shirts, hats, stuffed toys, and a million other elfin trappings capture our hearts. It is flattering and reassuring to receive word from the mother-to-be that she loves that little music box or snuggly blanket as much as you do.

Dear Connie and Lewis,

Thank you so much for the baby carrier. It's exactly what I wanted, down to the blue-and-white stripes. Ben and I can hardly wait to use it.

It was great to see both of you again, and we very much look forward to another terrific visit after the baby's born.

With much affection,

Liz

Dear Aunt Lydia,

The little silver cup is the most adorable thing I've ever seen. I don't want to give it to the baby at all. Instead I want to keep it next to the bed, where I can gaze upon it for hours and dream about the enchanted life I'll lead once the baby arrives. Tom says he'll probably end up using the cup himself (for a drink of that nice Scotch you gave him last Christmas), when my waters break. Thank you for the beautiful, beautiful cup.

Best love,

Ella

Dear Phyllis and Ken,

Your gift certificate for a year of diaper service came just in time! How can
we ever thank you? You have taken a terrific load off our shoulders and
given us more freedom to enjoy the baby, instead of worrying about how we'll
afford all those diapers. . . .

Rod and I will be forever indebted to you. Perhaps we can demonstrate some
of our gratitude, however, by inviting you to a viewing of Le Petit Prince some-
time next week, say, Thursday? Please say you'll stay for dinner and dessert.

Love,

Anna

For Birthday, Holiday, and Wedding Anniversary Gifts

Instead of sending a store-bought thank-you card for a special gift,
write a note that expresses your delight and appreciation in a much
more personal way. People love to be told that they've sent the ideal
gift; it makes them feel that their insights about who you are and
what you like are on target.

Dear Theo,

I couldn't believe what UPS delivered yesterday afternoon. What I mean is,
I never suspected that such a big box might contain such a small box that

might contain anything so beautiful or so rare or so perfect as my new ear-rings. They are exquisite. Thank you for reading my heart so clearly. I will always cherish these perfect gems, which I will wear with special pride, remembering that they came from you.

Love,

Katherine

For Hospitality

A while back, "bread-and-butter" letters were written to acknowledge the hospitality received at the home of a friend (usually for a weekend or more), and referred to the bread and butter the host provided. Even now, when so many people rely on the telephone to thank friends for a weekend visit or dinner invitation, it still feels good—and makes a wonderful impression on your host—to write a note of thanks.

Dear Amanda,

I can't remember the last time I felt so pampered and coddled. Everything about my visit was perfect, especially the time spent with you. The beach, the barbecued shrimp, and the margaritas were heavenly, too—but your husband deserves to be canonized for taking us on that heart-stopping sail around the sound! I'm afraid the "Q" train to 57th Street just doesn't compare.

Thank you for giving me such a wonderful break from the city. I enjoyed every minute of it.

Most affectionately yours,

Margaret

Dear Mr. and Mrs. Winter,

Nigel and I thank you for including us among your dinner guests Saturday evening. It was great fun to meet so many of our new neighbors. We especially enjoyed getting to know both of you a little better, and hope we can lure you to our dinner table, as soon as we've unearthed it.

The dinner was delicious, and Nigel has been pressuring me on a nightly basis to discover the secret to your incredibly delectable flan.

Thank you for making us feel as if we've always lived in our new neighborhood. Nothing, surely, can feel any better than this.

Cordially yours,

Susan and Nigel Grant

For Special Favors

A verbal "thank you" is sufficient for most everyday favors, such as borrowing a neighbor's ladder for the afternoon, or using a friend's car for a quick trip to the supermarket. But if a friend or neighbor goes out of the way to do something special for you or a member of your family, one of the most memorable ways to show your appreciation is to write a note of thanks.

Dear Jeanette,

Now that Liza is back from Northampton—glowing, excited, and full of plans—I'd like to thank you for taking the time to escort her from one college to another. It made a terrific difference for Liza to stay with such a good friend, and one who also knows the area as well as you do. She was full of praises for your boundless energy and inexhaustible good humor.

Liza was also immensely flattered (although she didn't say as much to me, but I couldn't help picking up on it) that you treated her as an equal, never condescending to her age. She couldn't get over the beautiful room you'd prepared for her and she loved having her own bathroom and keys to the house. Thank you, Jeanette, for treating Liza as if she were your own. But I'm warning you . . . if that girl gets admitted to Amherst next fall she's going to adopt you!

Love,

Jo

Dear Mr. Lloyd,

Thank you for looking after our puppy while we were in Atlanta for the funeral.

We would be so pleased and happy if you accepted the enclosed tickets to the garden show as a thank you for taking such wonderful care of our baby on so little notice. We thought the show might be of special interest to you this year, because the focus will be on composting and soil enrichment—two subjects you seem to know more about than anyone else on the planet. Charlie and I hope very much to see you at the show.

Sincerely,

Becky and Charlie Gorman

For Acts of Kindness

These days, when letters are so rare, the feelings expressed in them seem to take on extra power. Even in the 1850s when letter writing was a vital, everyday activity, the arrival of a particularly sympathetic letter could still elicit wonder and a deep feeling of gratitude: "And thank you for my dear letter," Emily Dickinson wrote to a friend, "which came on Saturday night, when all the world was still; thank you for the love it bore me, and for its golden thoughts, and feelings so like gems, that I was sure I gathered them in whole baskets of pearls!"

It is nothing short of a blessing to receive an act of kindness, especially when it comes at an unhappy, chaotic, or distressing time.

It is very important to acknowledge this special form of generosity with a note of thanks:

Dear Viv,

The last few months have felt so strange, and brought so many unforeseen urgencies, that I have hardly acknowledged the one beacon that has lighted so many dark hours with such tender constancy. I cannot begin to say how much your friendship and thoughtfulness have meant to me. I'm sure I could not have survived at all had you not appeared—always when I needed help the most—to look after the boys, or make a meal, or sit by my side for hours on end (like the angel I'm quite sure you must be). Even when I was at my worst, I was profoundly aware of your presence; the touch of your hand was enough to remind me that I was still rooted in life.

I don't think there are words strong enough or good enough to fully express my thanks, but they will forever be imprinted on my heart.

All my love,

Natalie

Dear Mrs. Granger,

At Lily's recital last month, I could literally hear the hope and confidence she has gained under your tutelage. I cannot begin to thank you for restoring these treasures to her, nor can I express adequately the feelings that overwhelmed me, as I listened to her play with such obvious pleasure.

Thanks to you, Lily's newfound musical confidence is spilling into the classroom, where she now participates with interest and fervor, and into our home, where she is so much happier. A mere "thank you" is far too feeble an expression of my gratitude for all that you have given us.

Sincerely,

Carol Fletcher

For Letters of Condolence

A letter of condolence can bring inestimable comfort when it is needed most. After Jane Austen's death, her sister, Cassandra, wrote a memorable thank-you note to Fanny Knight, whose letters had both touched and entertained her sister in the last few months of her life: "My dearest Fanny," she wrote. "Doubly dear to me now for her dear sake whom we have lost. She did love you most sincerely, and never shall I forget the proofs of love you gave her during her illness in writing those kind, amusing letters at a time when I know your feelings would have dictated so different a style. . . . "

It is surprisingly gratifying to receive condolence letters, even from people you don't know particularly well; very often their expressions of sympathy and support can mean almost as much to you as those of closer friends and family.

Although it is customary to mail thank-you notes for flowers and letters of condolence within a few weeks after receiving them, no one should expect a reply before the recipient is ready to respond.

However, the act of writing a reply to a note of condolence can be therapeutic; it encourages you to articulate thoughts and feelings that might never have been expressed otherwise. The person who receives your thank-you note will be reassured that an essential and deeply human experience has been acknowledged and shared.

The only real requirement for this kind of note is that it spring from the heart. It can be very short or rather long, depending on your preference and relationship to the person to whom you are writing. For example, to a very close friend you might write:

Dear Tess,

Your letter meant more to me than I can say. Dad's death was so sudden that I felt unexpectedly cut adrift—not only from him, but from my own past. Since Mom died, Dad has been my sole family connection. Now that he is dead, I feel that my childhood has vanished, and that part of my own memory has been erased forever. Your letter made me feel so much less at sea by anchoring me in your own fond memories of the times we shared together with Dad.

It is a great comfort to know that I am not completely alone in grieving for my father. Thank you for showing me how willing you are to share the burden of that grief, as well as the joy of remembering who he was and what fun we had together, especially the last few winters in Key West, when he was at his best. I will never forget what you have done to help me realize how much of my dad is still alive in me—and always will be. At the same time I feel very strongly that I have gained a sister in you, the one I thought I'd never have. This is truly an unexpected joy.

Love,

Emma

To a friend

Dear Beth,

Thank you for your thoughtful note.

Your offer of help is more generous than I can say. Please know that you are the first person I would ever call if I thought there was anything anyone could do. Right now, though, I feel the need to close the shutters for a while. Knowing that you are "out there" ready to welcome me back is a great comfort, and I am deeply thankful for your friendship.

Very sincerely,

Trish

To a neighbor or acquaintance

Dear Mrs. Cummings,

Thank you for all your kindness at the time of my mother's death.

Your thoughtful words and beautiful pink roses were deeply appreciated by all of us.

Sincerely yours,

Selma McBain

To colleagues,
business associates, or clients

Dear Mr. Levin,

It was very kind of you, and all of Mother's good friends on the editorial staff, to send the tulip windowbox. I have never seen anything prettier, and I know Mother would have adored it.

On behalf of my family, I thank you for honoring her memory with the flowers she loved best, and for sending such thoughtful and moving expressions of sympathy. We are grateful to you for every one of them; your extraordinary letters have shown us exactly why Mother was so pleased to work with all of you for so many happy years.

Sincerely,

Willa Swenson

Acknowledgment of a condolence letter

Dear Mrs. Donnell,

Mother asked me to write to you, as she cannot do so herself at the moment.

She would like you to know how very much she appreciated your kind letter and the beautiful pot of white peonies you sent her. She promises to write to you herself, as soon as she can. In the meantime, Mother has asked me to send you her love.

Sincerely yours,
Molly

For Letters of Congratulation

It is a delightful shock to receive a personal letter instead of a store-bought card on a special occasion. To receive a handwritten note of congratulation seems all the more miraculous when you consider how many stunning commercial cards are available for every conceivable occasion. Yet, the message inside a store-bought card can never be as personal as the one you write yourself.

Writing a note of thanks in return can be lots of fun. Relax, and let your thoughts and good feelings roll off your pen. Remember, you're writing to someone you know and like—which gives you lots of freedom to be as nostalgic, silly, newsy, or earnest as you like.

Dear Tony,

I can't believe you remembered!

Even though I pretend to be completely blasé about my birthday, I'm always pleased whenever it's acknowledged.

Thank you so much for the wonderful letter. I put off reading it until the moment was exactly right: after work, with my feet up, and a big glass of wine in hand. Here's to you. I couldn't have asked for a nicer present on my birthday.

With much affection,

Jane

On a marriage

Dear Mrs. Lowell,

Thank you very much for your lovely note of congratulation. Todd and I appreciate your good wishes for the future—which will be much brighter, I might add, if you promise to visit us as soon as possible. We are eager to show off our very nice, brand-new apartment while it is still clean. So please come right away. We promise to have lots of coffee and goodies on hand.

With great fondness,

Your old neighbor, Irene (Phillips) Abernathy

On a wedding anniversary

Dear Peg,

Has it really been twenty-five years? Adam and I still feel like the kids we were when we got married. It doesn't seem possible that our own children have landed in college already, or that they're busily earning degrees in esoteric subjects. (Sound familiar?) Do you suppose it's too late for us to consider grad school? What about an advanced degree in puff pastry or bullfighting?

Thank you for your wonderful letter, and for reminding us of all the good times we've had over the last twenty-five years. I've got to agree with Adam, though, when he says, "It wouldn't have been nearly as much fun if Margaret hadn't been along for the ride."

Lots of love,

Sarah

On the birth of a child

Dear Mrs. Greene,

Thank you for all your good wishes for little Jessie, who, incredibly, will be one month old tomorrow. Brad and I still can't quite believe she's here, after so many months of waiting and worrying and wondering. We are idiotically happy, and deeply appreciate your congratulations.

Sincerely,

Nancy Freeman

On graduating

Dear Dr. Fowles,

It made me happy to receive your wonderful letter. You are right about all the excitement at home. I don't think my parents have recovered from the recent shock of my parole from college. Mother in particular keeps asking me if there isn't some course I've tucked away that needs to be completed before I'm really "done." And Dad keeps scratching his head and wondering how his nice little girl ever got interested in anything as macabre as forensic medicine.

I was very flattered and pleased by your offer to introduce me to Dr. Fiori of the Medical Examiner's Office. Even if there is no internship in the offing this summer, it will have been a great honor to meet Dr. Fiori and his staff. Thank you for making these arrangements, and for taking such an enthusiastic interest in my fledgling career. I am deeply grateful.

Sincerely,

Natalie Carr

Letters of Congratulation

If you hear of a friend's good news—whether it's a marriage, the birth of a child, an auspicious career change, or a special honor—sit down right away and fire off a jubilant little note. If it is written promptly, your letter of congratulation will sound as exuberant and as sincere as you feel. If you wait too long to respond to the occasion, however, your message may lack the candor and cheer this sort of note is meant to communicate.

Just like any other form of social correspondence, a letter of congratulation has a specific purpose: to share the joy of a happy occasion. When writing notes of this kind, try not to introduce extraneous subjects, and steer away from feelings and thoughts that might cast a dark shadow over your friend's happiness.

Although letters of congratulation are never required, they help deepen friendships, fortify family connections, and lend a personal touch to business relationships. They may be brief and formal, or chatty and casual—depending on the occasion and how well you know the recipient.

On announcement of engagement

Although it is customary to congratulate the man—never the woman—on his engagement (the woman is sent "good wishes for her happiness"), one may follow whatever style comes with the greatest ease. As long as the letter expresses sincere happiness in sharing the joy of the occasion, it is fulfilling its purpose. This task should be an easy and pleasurable one, especially if the recipients are good friends. Relax and enjoy the opportunity to bask in their good fortune.

Dear Kathleen,

It was wonderful to receive your note telling me about your engagement to Ted Parker. Please give my congratulations to Ted, who is about to gain the most wonderful (not to mention brilliant and beautiful) woman in the world as his wife. Don't forget to take every opportunity to remind him how lucky he is. I am immensely pleased, Kathleen, by your obvious joy in having made the decision to marry a man who has already made you so content. I send you both my warmest good wishes for every happiness in your life together.

Meantime, I hope you and Ted will accept an invitation to have dinner with me at Chanterelle so we can officially celebrate this marvelous occasion. I'll phone soon to make a date.

Always affectionately,
Aunt Beatrice

On a marriage

Although it is the custom to address a note of congratulation to both the bride and the groom, a note may be written to the bride or to the groom individually. It all depends on the nature of your friendship: whether you know the bride and groom equally well, or if one of the couple is better known to you than the other. In either case, writing a note of this kind can be great fun.

Dear Judith,

Who'd have thought you'd end up like this: a respected matron and a veritable pillar of the community. Does this mean we can't be seen clinging half-naked to your little Sunfish next summer? And what about our annual vineyard crawl?

Actually, I'm very happy about your marriage to Ian. I've known him for a million years, as you know. He's a good man, and I can't think of a nicer husband for you (except if you married me, of course). So please accept my most sincere congratulations and best wishes for every happiness.

Fondly,

Your friend, Craig

On a wedding anniversary

Dear Ted and Kathleen,

I was astonished when Henry told me that your fifth anniversary is next month. It is so unlike him to be on top of this sort of thing, which only shows how crazy he is (as I am, too) about both of you. Congratulations. Here's to many, many more years of happiness. You deserve every one of them.

Love,

Eve and Henry

On the birth of a child

Is any occasion happier or more exciting than the arrival of a baby, except, perhaps, the arrival of another baby? No matter how many of them show up, it is very difficult to find their presence either boring or predictable.

A good way to let a mother know how happy you are at the arrival of her baby is to send a short, or even a very long and chatty, note of congratulation. After all she's been through, it will be a great source of comfort, joy, and amusement to know that other adults are as eager to welcome her newborn as she is.

Dear Kathleen,

I am writing to you on this momentous occasion because Henry is incapable of giving any sort of assistance. I'm afraid he is in a state of profound nerves, after staying up half the night waiting to hear the good news of young Jasper's arrival. At the moment Henry is frantically searching the house for a corkscrew (an absurd exercise; anyone who has spent more than eleven minutes here knows that a corkscrew can be found virtually anywhere). Nevertheless, the plan is to uncork a very nice bottle of something. Glasses will be lifted in honor of young Jasper, whom we hope to meet very soon. If only Henry would stop bellowing about "the sanctity of it all" long enough to finish packing.

We are very proud of you, my dear, and very glad that Jasper has arrived exactly on schedule. This is a promising sign. None of the men in my family—Henry, least of all—was ever reliable about time.

Congratulations to both of you, Kathleen and Ted. We are insanely happy for you and send our best love.

As ever,

Eve and Henry

On a birthday

These days, commercial birthday cards are ubiquitous. They practically leap at you from bulging displays in card shops, bookstores, supermarkets, and fancy boutiques. Collecting and browsing for cards has become a legitimate pastime and can even offer Zen-like satisfactions. Card-store epiphanies are not unknown: It is uncanny how appropriate some preprinted messages are for some of the people we know. There's no denying the usefulness and beauty of commercial cards. They provide a friendly, casual way to congratulate acquaintances and colleagues on their birthdays.

Illustrated blank cards are a boon to writers who have the time to compose a personal message, rather than rely on ready-made congratulations. Still, there is nothing like receiving a letter, no matter how short, on one's birthday. The rarity of such a communication gives it all the qualities of a special gift.

FOR ADDRESS ONLY

Mr. E. Shepherd St.
#66 walnut St.
Lebanon Tenn

chapter six.

Dear friends. 2-21-11

letter reci'd, & was
glad to hear from you
ance. it soon.
we having a nice
n storm all are well
+ hope you are both the
am washing today
u circle, & think

The Comfort of Connection

Condolence and Sympathy Letters

Yet write, oh write me all, that I may join
Griefs to thy griefs, and echo sighs to thine.

Alexander Pope,

"Eloisa to Abelard"

No other form of correspondence is as deeply affecting or can say as much in so few words as a condolence letter. It may require a little more effort to write than a thank-you note, but your words will be appreciated more than you can imagine. A friend has often said that the condolence letters she received after her husband died helped sustain her for months and even years after his death.

It seems incredible that a few pieces of paper can offer so much solace, and yet they do. Condolence letters give you an almost palpable feeling that the people closest to you have not only acknowledged your pain, but have given it deep consideration. It is immeasurably soothing to know that you are in someone's thoughts. Madame de Sévigné referred to this form of love—for surely it must be love—as "habitual thought": "If you think of me," she once wrote to her daughter, "rest assured that I think constantly of you."

Mourning the death of someone you love can be a profoundly isolating experience, but letters can help break the spell. The powerful subtext of a condolence letter is: You are not alone. Yet, as important as this message is, it can be expressed in just a few simple words. "One who only said 'I am sorry' helped me the most," Emily Dickinson wrote after her father's death.

Most of us approach writing condolence letters with more than a little anxiety, but it always helps to envision the person to whom you are writing. As soon as you focus your thoughts on what that person is experiencing and feeling, it is easier to let go of your concerns about "saying the right thing." No matter how homespun, your own words are always best: "I was so surprised to receive a note from Peter," a friend said shortly after her mother's funeral. "He's so busy and I know how nervous he gets about writing anything, but it made me feel good—just knowing he'd taken the time to write." Peter's letter was only two lines long, but it was written from his heart and did exactly what a condolence letter should do: express affection and support for someone who needs it very much.

One of the greatest consolations of receiving a letter of condolence is knowing that the message it contains will never grow dim or lose its power to reassure and encourage. "Letters were good company after the funeral," a friend wrote. "Everyone went home to pick up the pieces of their lives, but I felt as if mine had been blown sky-high. I sat in bed for hours and read letters over and over again." Unlike a conversation, whether in person or over the telephone, a letter can be held close; it contains a breath of life. When you hold a letter in your hands you can envision the writer sitting at her desk or kitchen table and writing on the same piece of paper. It is a lovely feeling of connection, as if it wouldn't take more than crossing the room and walking through a door to be in the presence of a caring friend.

Condolence letters are personal. The most affecting ones are simple and true; they express what you feel not only about the man or woman who has died, and what the loss of their life means to you, but they also acknowledge how much that man or woman meant to the bereaved.

This thoughtful letter, which was written to a friend after her husband died, is a powerful and moving affirmation of the mourner's experience:

Dear Gail,

I imagine you have heard so many stories about Jerry's generosity, his relentless interest and curiosity. And I imagine that you more than anyone knew his vulnerability.

I was one of the many people fortunate to receive his nurturance, his kindness, and sympathy. Jerry was a pivotal figure in many of our lives. I am grateful because he taught me something about the necessity for courage—and generosity—to sustain one's creativity.

Jerry spoke of you with such love and devotion. I cannot imagine what this loss is for you but please know that I send you my sympathy and deep admiration. I believe Jerry could not have given so much of himself to others without you there in his life.

Very truly yours,

Linda

Emily Dickinson understood how particularly painful was the loss of a beloved spouse. When a good friend's husband died, she wrote: "I hasten to you, Mary, because no moment must be lost when a heart is breaking." In the same note Dickinson acknowledged her friend's response to one she had written earlier: "I am glad," she said, "if the broken words helped you. I had not hoped so much, I felt so faint in uttering them, thinking of your great pain." Dickinson's willingness to share Mary's grief was a tremen-

The birds that father rescued are trifling in his trees. How flippant are the saved! They were even frolicking at his grave, when Vinnie went there yesterday. Nature must be too young to feel, or many years too old.

Emily Dickinson to Louise and Frances Norcros

dous proof of her affection, and one that undoubtedly strength-
ened their devotion to each other.

∞

Sharing the Memory of a Loved One

Nothing can ever give back a life, but a condolence letter can help
reconstruct it. Each time you make a conscious effort to remember
and share memories of the people you love, you give them a more
permanent place in the continuum of life. You need never feel shy
about writing candidly or intimately about someone who has died.
Remembering and telling stories is a way of dispelling the dreadful
sense that people simply vanish when they die, without leaving a
trace. Very shortly after her father's death, a friend and her family
gathered around the dinner table to share each other's company and
exchange memories of their father. Someone lightly referred to the
meal as "the last supper" because they all were planning to return to
their own homes in different parts of the country the following day.
But nothing irreverent was meant. If anything, the atmosphere
around the table that night was charged with what can only be
described as a kind of loving lightness, a joyful willingness to
remember and embrace all the special qualities of a life that would
never be forgotten.

When you acknowledge the special qualities of a relationship that has been torn in two by a death, you return something quite valuable to the surviving "half": "I have thought so much of you, since Madge's death," Virginia Woolf wrote to Janet Vaughan. " . . . I had a long letter from her last summer, which was full of you, and the pleasure you gave her. She seemed so happy with you." Virginia Woolf knew instinctively how vulnerable love makes us and how important it is to feel mutual belonging in a relationship. Her letter must have given Janet the confirmation she craved.

At another time, Woolf wrote to the husband of her close friend Vita Sackville-West, whose father had just died. It is a very short letter but a poignant one because it is so simple, clear, and specific:

My dear Harold,

Would you let me know if there were anything you think I could do for Vita? I'm afraid there isn't, but if there were, nothing would give me greater happiness, as you know, and I am perfectly free.

I'm so glad I knew Lord Sackville enough to feel his great charm and sweetness. I loved seeing him and Vita together.

With deep affection,

Yours,
Virginia

When to Write

It is never too soon, nor is it ever too late, to extend sympathy and understanding to those who are grieving. Acknowledging loss over a period of time affirms the process of grieving; it conveys the understanding that, for the bereaved, mourning doesn't simply end after the formal rituals stop—it lives and changes shape over time:

It was very gratifying and it helped me a great deal to hear from friends in the year after Martin's death. When the funeral was over I felt as if I had fallen into a silent chasm, where there was simply no conversation about his death. In an odd way, it made me feel as if Martin was a subject that shouldn't be discussed. People are sometimes a little cruel in their kindness: I feel sure the general thinking was that any conversation about him might be too painful for me, when all I really wanted to do was to talk and talk about Martin. . . . Letters from friends, and the ones I wrote back to them, were a tremendous relief. At last I could feel that I wasn't making other people feel uncomfortable whenever I spoke of Martin or the grief I still feel.

Another friend, who has also experienced the death of someone she loves, makes a special point of sending notes on a regular basis to friends who are bereaved. "I see it as an essential aspect of friendship," she says. "I make lots of phone calls to my friends to check up on them, but when I really want to say what's in my heart I write it down, even if it's just a few words." Going to your mailbox and finding a friendly note among all the impersonal bills and noisy advertisements makes you feel that the world isn't completely indifferent to your grief.

Losing a Parent

The death of a parent is probably our most commonly shared experience of death—and it is always a powerful loss. Losing your connection to the very life that gave you breath and life is a profound experience, with many repercussions. It can be particularly uprooting if a parent's death leaves one orphaned. "I keep expecting to hear her voice when the phone rings," a friend says of her late mother. "I feel that her death has left me without a living connection to my own childhood. Now that I have a daughter of my own, I feel my mother's absence more acutely than ever. I am so sorry that my child will never have the chance to meet her—I mean, meet my past, my starting point, where I began." The sense of being cut adrift in the world, without recourse to one's own past, is profoundly unsettling. Long after both of her parents were dead, Colette wrote to a friend on the eve of her brother's death: "Now he will take with him our childhood past, and an irreplaceable cluster of memories which he has kept and classified. When he is gone, I'll no longer have anyone

Mama died the day before yesterday. I don't want to go to the burial. I shall wear no visible mourning, and I am telling almost no one. But I am tormented by the stupid notion that I shall no longer be able to write to her as I always have.

Colette to Léon Hamel

to consult as to what happened." Sadly, there is no insurance against loss of this kind, but even the shortest note can celebrate and preserve an important piece of the past. Writing about a parent who has died honors his or her memory while keeping it safe from the predations of time. "If you write down minutely what you remember of her from your earliest years," Samuel Johnson wrote to a friend who had lost his mother, "you will read it with great pleasure, and receive from it many hints of soothing recollection, when time shall remove her yet farther from you, and your grief shall be matured to veneration."

No human circumstance went unobserved or unfelt by Emily Dickinson. In the letter she wrote to her newly orphaned cousins, Dickinson's voice is so near you can almost feel the warmth of her breath: "What shall I tell these darlings except that my father and mother are half their father and mother, and my home half theirs, whenever, and for as long as, they will."

On the day her own mother died, Dickinson wrote the briefest of notes to her friend Maria Whitney:

Sweet Friend,

Our Mother ceased—

While we bear her dear form through the Wilderness, I am sure you are with us.

Emily

On the Death of a Child

Nothing is more unthinkable or heartbreaking than the death of a child, yet when it occurs, it is of the utmost importance to communicate as much compassion and understanding as can possibly be expressed in writing.

There should be nothing in a note of this kind that might bring even the slightest degree of pain to the parents; and there should never be any mention whatsoever of the child's suffering. References to, or questions about, how a child has died are cruelly painful to parents whose hearts have been riven. Solace, support, and the reassurance of love is what these notes  must communicate. Focus on what the parents are feeling, not on yourself, and concentrate on expressing your sympathy as simply and sincerely as possible.

It may seem terribly inadequate to send a mere note to people who have lost a child, but doing so is worth it if your words bring even a very small, fleeting moment of comfort.

Practical but essential matters tend to slip away from those who are profoundly bereaved. Under these circumstances, it is thoughtful to ask if you can be of use. However, do not volunteer to help if you cannot come through with your offer.

The following letters were written from two points of view, but hopefully they give a sense of the feeling one wants to convey in a letter of this kind:

Dear Ms. Sinclair,

I hope you will forgive us for intruding on your grief. Jim and I very much enjoyed meeting you and your husband this summer at the retreat in Bar Harbor. Although we haven't had much time to become well acquainted, I must tell you how very deeply we feel for you.

We know only too well what you must be going through. It has been only two years since our daughter, Sophie, died.

Our hearts are full of sympathy for you both. Please call us, if we can help. We'd like to.

Most sincerely yours,

Nina and Jim Bascomb

Dear Pam,

I can't tell you how sorry I am, but please know that I'm thinking of you with all my heart—and that I'll always be here for you, if you want to talk. Please call me. Anytime.

I send all my love to you and Allan.

Yours, as ever,

Elizabeth

Don't cry, dear Mary. Let us do that for you, because you are too tired now. We don't know how dark it is, but if you are at sea, perhaps when we say that we are there, you won't be as afraid. The waves are very big, but every one that covers you, covers us, too.

Dear Mary, you can't see us, but we are close at your side. May we comfort You?

Emily Dickinson to Mrs. Samuel Bowles (Three of Mrs. Bowles's children were stillborn. This note may have been written after the third stillbirth.)

∽

A Gift of Comfort

Unfortunately, there are many circumstances in our lives that cause anguish. In almost all cases, however, whether it's death, divorce, or illness, a letter of sympathy and support is one of the most powerful gifts we can give or receive. Just letting a friend know that he or she is in your heart and in your thoughts is a healing gesture. If you carefully consider the person to whom you are writing, it is never too difficult to express yourself truthfully; warmth and concern never fail to touch another's heart.

Below are various circumstances under which a letter of sympathy or condolence might be written, as well as a few suggestions about what to keep in mind as you write them.

Divorce

Though it's often best not to initiate any special communication when you hear the news of a friends or a relative's divorce or separation, it is important to get in touch right away, once he or she has told you about it.

Separation and divorce can have a devastating effect on friendship, especially if you have been close to both the husband and the wife. Generally, a good friend will not ask you to take sides, but no matter how fair everyone tries to be, it is extremely difficult not to get entangled in the details. When you do write, focus your thoughts on your friend's state of mind, and, if you can, on immediate ways to help relieve sorrow, anger, suffering, or a sense of defeat. Sometimes a good friend simply needs to hear that your love and support are still in place, despite public censure and everybody's "bad" behavior. Just saying, "I'm so sorry!" and "You can count on me, no matter what—I'm here for you," can make a tremendous difference for a friend who is most likely feeling abandoned or misunderstood.

This letter was received by a friend when she was going through a difficult breakup. She has often said how much she appreciated her friend's generosity:

Dear Cass,

I wish I could crawl into your pocket so you wouldn't feel quite so alone. I can't imagine the pain you've been through. I'm so sorry that things have come to an impasse with Stephan, but you mustn't blame yourself.

I think you've made a very good decision to put a little distance between yourself and the sad events of the last few months. You have such a big heart and so much more sense than just about anyone I know, that I feel sure you will do exactly the right thing.

I trust that you know how deeply I care for you, and how much pleasure it would give me if there were anything I could do. . . . Please let me know.

All my love,

Christina

Friendships and family relationships are so complicated and personal that it is virtually impossible to offer a formula or specific suggestions for every letter we write. The only rule of thumb is to be as receptive, sincere, and responsive as possible in your correspondence. When there is a misfortune or calamity in a friend's life, it isn't always important to know the reasons why, or to make judgments. What is important is to stay in touch—the best way you know how.

Illness

If you can capture on paper what you would do or say while visiting a sick friend, your efforts will go a long way toward giving him or her a few moments of comfort. Hospitalization can be an isolating experience, but letters help bring the world to a friend's bedside.

Get-well notes are really nothing more than hugs on paper, but they contribute more than you might think to sustaining the good spirits and optimistic outlook we all need to get better.

Much has been said and written about the curative powers of laughter, so never worry about exercising your sense of humor when you write to a friend.

Dear Monica,

I was so sorry to hear of your illness. Everyone at work is agitating wildly for your return. No one is having any fun at all without you, so hurry up and get better.

I've enclosed an un-put-downable paperback, which has now made the rounds at work. We thought you'd love it, too, and that it might take your mind off all the solicitous interns we've seen swanning over to your bedside every few minutes. So pay attention. There will be a quiz.

Very sincerely yours,

Deborah

P.S. Please let me know when you'd like visitors again. I'd love to see you.

Letters to the family on the death of a friend

Condolence letters written to the family of a friend who has died can be especially insightful for the parents: Hearing from an adult child's peers and friends gives them a broader sense of who their child was. Parents are naturally curious about their own children, who, from the time they enter the first grade, seem to lead interesting, if mysterious, lives of their own. Letters from an adult child's friends help fill in the blanks as well as supply solace of a very special sort: A parent's love is immediate, complete, and irrevocable, but a friend's love is earned. Hearing all about the different ways their child was loved and appreciated by others increases the store of their own affection and adds immeasurably to the memory of the one they so loved.

Dear Mr. and Mrs. Eastman,

I'm writing to you about Beatrice because I don't know what else to do, and because I know how much she loved you and how much you loved her.

I loved Beatrice, too, but perhaps for different reasons than you might think. It is true that I loved her for the passion she brought to her work— she was a powerful and tactful lobbyist, if you can imagine such a paradox! Beatrice will be missed and mourned by hundreds of her colleagues and supporters, but I will miss her for other, far less public reasons.

I will miss the twin white stripes in her hair that gave Beatrice the look of an inquisitive, but very affectionate badger. I will miss the way

she could pull an apartment together with an artful toss of a cushion. I will miss the habit she had of resting her hand on my arm when she wanted to tell me something important, or if I was feeling bad. I will miss the way her eyes would come swimming up over the top of her glasses whenever she looked up suddenly. She was an inexhaustible cross-country skier. She loaned money to friends when they needed it, and didn't have a single cruel sinew or bone in her body. She kept everyone's plants alive. She was my best friend.

Beatrice said any special qualities she had came from you. You were the people she looked up to and admired. She was one of the few friends I have who never seemed to mind hearing long messages from her parents on the answering machine. She worried about you and talked about "being there" as you grew older. She thought you should get a new car—a safer, "heavier" one. She was planning to fly out for your fortieth anniversary. She would have been there on the eighteenth.

There is nothing more—and a million more things I could say about Beatrice. But there is nothing I can say, I'm sure, to help lessen the pain of her absence. She leaves too huge a void in our lives to fill with anything but sorrow, but Beatrice would have hated that, would have wanted us to make an effort. That's what this letter is, an attempt to reach you and to say how much I'm thinking of you and how heavy my heart is for you—not only with the pain of her loss, but with all the love she left for us. After all, that's the thing that will survive, no matter what.

With kindest thoughts for you both,

Sincerely,

Olivia Rowe

Never Hesitate to Write

In the end, writing a condolence letter is an active, concrete way to relieve the feelings of frustration and powerlessness that often overwhelm family and friends who are desperate to do something for the bereaved. At the same time, even the briefest letter can bring a surprising and heartening measure of comfort to those in mourning.

Even if you have never experienced the death of someone you

love, it is still possible to write a thoughtful and caring letter of condolence. All it requires is your empathy. If you write as simply and naturally as you can about what you are feeling at the moment, your words will convey all the sympathy and under-standing you truly feel. To write a condolence letter is to make a gift of love, which, surely, is the best medicine of all for a broken heart.

Dear Madam,

Allow me to assure you and Mr. Thrale that I very sincerely regret your present affliction, and very sincerely wish it were in my power to alleviate it. Were you as sure as I am of my concern for you, I doubt not that it would be some relief. You have now with you Dr. Johnson, whose friendship is the most effectual consolation under heaven. I wish not to intrude upon you; but as soon as you let me know that my presence will not be troublesome, I shall hasten to your house, where as I have shared much happiness, I would willingly bear a part in mourning.

I ever am, Madam,
Your obliged humble servant,
James Boswell
(Written on the occasion of the death of the Thrales' only son)

chapter seven

Staying in Touch with the World

Letters of Admiration, Letters of Complaint, Letters to Magazines, Alumnae Newsletters, and More

For most of us, the phrase "letter-writing" usually evokes images of long, delightful personal letters, but other forms of correspondence can satisfy our craving for connection as well. These letters may not be as intimate or informal as the ones we write to close friends and family, but they link us to the world in dynamic and satisfying ways nonetheless. Very often there is a deeply human "payoff" to the letters we write in response to editorials or even job interviews. These letters give us a surprising range of opportunities in which to express ourselves with feeling and conviction.

When you write a letter to the editor of a newspaper, for example, you do something more than merely express an opinion: You take your place in the world. "Staking a claim" might be the more vigorous term for it, but in any case, the expression of a personal opinion is just as important an act of connection as it is to vote, or, for that matter, to commit yourself to a meaningful personal relationship. No matter how elusive or complex a public concern or debate may be, it always helps to "put a human face" on it.

When you write an admiring letter to an author, you reinforce the idea that a book is a dialogue, and that your voice is an important part of the conversation. At the same time, the act of writing itself helps clarify and deepen your own thoughts about a specific work. A letter affirms that there is someone on the other side of a book, not just a "he," "she," or a "them." Sometimes an exchange of letters evolves into a friendship that might never have formed under other circumstances. Henry Miller and Lawrence Durrell met because of a fan letter, and so did Francine du Plessix Gray and Joyce Carol Oates. A friend tells a story about two people she knows well who were once strangers to each other. Both are painters: One lives on the East Coast, the other on the West. At a gallery opening in SoHo, the East Coast artist fell in love with the work of the West Coast artist and wrote him an admiring postcard on an impulse, never suspecting for a moment that they would eventually meet and become close friends.

Emily Dickinson once wrote a letter to the author of an article she read in the pages of *The Atlantic Monthly*. By the time she received a letter in return, an inextinguishable friendship had been kindled.

It is very gratifying to feel linked to the world outside your own front door. Dickinson overcame what might have become a particularly hermetic form of isolation by choosing to communicate her thoughts and feelings through verse. Each one of us is given the choice of how to find her own "letter to the world." The joy of it is that you don't have to be an accomplished poet to find the process rewarding. Every letter is a creative act that has the potential to bridge almost any distance or difference of opinion. Each one brings us closer to an understanding of ourselves and the world around us.

A Personal Touch

Sometimes the very idea of writing a business letter can make you feel so tense that you can't hear the natural rhythm of your own thoughts and speech. Before you know it you're using borrowed phrases and dull, stilted language—all in an effort to sound professional. More often than not the strain of creating an artificial letter is so exhausting that you end up with a boring, lifeless "document." But letters don't have to sound officious or impersonal to be taken seriously.

The best letters—no matter what kind—are conversational, interesting to read, and friendly in spirit. The right tone is remarkably easy to achieve if you remember that you are writing to a person, not to an Institution or a Multinational Corporation. If you can envision "someone warm and breathing on the other side of the page"—as Virginia Woolf advised—even your most businesslike letters will come alive with human interest.

Even the late John D. Rockefeller, Sr., whom one might expect to have had a more hard-edged philosophy toward business, once said that he would pay more for "the ability to deal with people . . . than any other purchasable commodity under the sun."

∞

Letters Mingle Souls

Some letters give back returns that are especially personal. Magazine columns, such as *Victoria's* "Dear Friends" and "Reader to Reader," offer wonderfully fertile opportunities for like-minded souls to share their wisdom and reflect on life's passages. These letters express a generous range of personal values—whether it's a feeling of connectedness, a sense of peace, the satisfactions of professional accomplishment, or a deep appreciation for beauty. In the same column that offers a letter celebrating the memory of a mother's love, there might be a very different expression of appreciation, such as the one Anna Bies wrote to *Victoria:*

Your August issue on entrepreneurs was very timely. I had been thinking about starting my own business but had been discouraged by family and friends. The stories of successful women following their dreams in business rekindled my own interest in starting mine. I was inspired and heartened to learn about so many who have taken a simple idea and made it blossom. Thank you so much.

Every time you sit down to write a letter to your favorite magazine, you widen the circle of friends around you. It doesn't matter if you've never met them before, especially when you have so much in common. The writer Jean Rhys once said that "all writing is a huge lake," and the only thing that matters "is feeding the lake." It must be the same for friendship.

Letters of Admiration

Reading a friendly letter from someone you've never met is like crossing the threshold of a particularly inviting room in a house you've always wanted to live in. Letters give us entry to others' lives; they can rescue us from isolation and give us hope. Elizabeth Barrett was a lonely invalid, whose published poems inspired a friendly and admiring letter from Robert Browning. In her own words, Barrett "pounced upon the opportunity of corresponding with the poet": "I thank you, dear Mr. Browning, from the bottom of my heart," she wrote. "Such a letter from such a hand." George Bernard

Shaw and the actress Ellen Terry wrote to each other for twenty-five years—a delightful friendship on paper that enriched both their lives; and Rilke, who admitted that much of his creative expression went into the letters he wrote, addressed *Letters to a Young Poet* to a correspondent he had never seen.

Of all the letters we write, fan letters are probably among the most spontaneous, for the simple reason that they are pure projections of our appreciation. We write fan letters because they give us a sense of proximity and connection to people we admire, and, perhaps, even love. At the same time, a fan letter is an enduring testament to excellence, which puts it in a category of its own—perhaps somewhere between a valentine and an honorary degree.

People who receive a lot of fan letters say the best ones are personal and affectionate, but serious and thoughtful, too: "It's always nice to know *why* someone admires your books as much as they do," says a successful author, "and it's especially nice if that person just happens to write books themselves." The implication is that praise from someone who sincerely understands and appreciates the nature of what you do is twice as sweet.

But you don't have to be a famous author to enjoy sending (or receiving) fan letters. You can write a letter of appreciation to anyone whose creativity or professionalism you admire. It's a wonderful way of showing your support, especially for people who work by themselves and who rarely receive feedback about their work.

A friend, who operates a small mail-order knitted-sweater business from her home, called recently to say that to her utter surprise and joy, she'd received a fan letter from a customer: "It is so satisfying to hear from someone who has such a strong and passionate sense of what I do," she said. "I'm definitely going to write back to her and see if we can't get together some time soon. . . . I have a hunch she's another wild and crazy knitter, just like me."

A few years ago, another friend, a biologist who does experimental work with DNA, wrote to a colleague whose work she admires. After corresponding for almost three years, they finally met at a conference. Now they write to each other with even more intensity and plan to collaborate on a number of projects.

At the very least, a fan letter can inspire more friendly conversation—either on paper or in person. But, even better, fan letters have the power to transform tenuous connections into strong partnerships and lasting friendships.

Every time you pick up your pen to make personal contact with someone you admire, but might never meet, you risk being misunderstood or even rejected. But take courage! Remember all the deep and lasting attachments that have been nourished on letters written by "pen pals"—strangers who eventually became dear friends.

∞

Rekindling Old Connections

A friend recently wrote to say that she'd read a wonderful letter in an alumnae newsletter from one of her college classmates, a woman she'd always admired and who had recently become a district attorney:

I can't believe it. There was a long letter from Maria S. in the Alumnae Quarterly. *I knew that she was doing spectacularly well as a lawyer, which makes me feel proud, of course. But part of me has always felt that she might disapprove of the hopelessly domestic and chaotic life I've been leading lately. . . . You know, hunting for tiny truck parts under Ben's bed and sewing tails back onto stuffed cats for Marjorie or Rebecca. Now I hear from Maria that her twins (!) keep her even busier than the courts ever did. Still, she says she can't help loving the mayhem at home, and wants to get in touch with other moms in our class. I'm so delighted and relieved that I'm going to sit down and write to her—just as soon as I can find that little tractor tire I've been looking for all morning.*

Glancing through the pages of our class news, we get occasional glimpses of friends we haven't seen in years, but with whom we still share a special bond. To some extent, each of their lives is a touchstone. We may have a tendency to measure our successes by theirs, but we also rejoice in news of their children; laugh at tales of vacations spent in haunted cottages; and nod in recognition when we read of a classmate's work in a difficult field, or her struggle with illness or divorce. Each letter tells a story we recognize as part of our own. A newsletter reminds us that we are still connected to each other, despite the passage of time and the vagaries of individual lives.

It is surprisingly easy, not to mention pleasurable, to "pick up" a friendship where it left off, even if it has been many years since you last saw or wrote a letter to a particular friend. What matters, in the end, is feeling good about renewing contact with someone you've always cared about. Your life is full of interesting and meaningful content, no matter how uneventful you might think it is. Writing about yourself is an act of courage . . . and half the adventure's in the telling. Even the great French biographer André Maurois admitted that "A well-written life will always be rarer than a well-spent one." When old friends read your letters, they will be delighted to hear your voice again and share your journey, no matter how different it may be from their own.

∞

Letters of Complaint

There are times when a phone call to a utility or credit card company is simply not enough to get the results you want: A letter needs to be written, but you keep putting it off because you feel intimidated by bureaucracy or mystified by business etiquette.

Whenever you feel unsure about writing these kinds of letters, it always helps to relax for a minute and focus on exactly what you want to accomplish. A letter is a lot easier to write, and is much more effective, if you have a specific thought or request to base it on. Next, make sure that the references you make, for example, dates, titles, spelling (especially the names of people, companies, and organizations), punctuation, and language are accurate. Be as thorough as possible; cover all the important points you want to make in a clear and straightforward way. Your letter can be as short and concise as you like, but don't forget to be cordial—even if you have a serious complaint.

Your main objective in writing a business letter—*especially* a letter of complaint—is to get the results you want. Avoid writing anything that might be misunderstood or cause distress. And don't write in anger: Later you may regret or be embarrassed by what you've said.

At the same time, a complaint letter doesn't have to be stiff or impersonal to be taken seriously. You can bring all the pleasures of writing with humor, interest, and humanity—even to the most serious letter of complaint.

Instead of making an angry phone call or writing a threatening letter to the president of a company that had recently renovated her kitchen, a friend wrote an amused, if mildly alarmed, account of a disaster that had occurred shortly after the last of the company's "experts" had gone home. She wrote:

I woke up from a sound sleep yesterday morning to a series of loud, snapping noises. We've lived in the country for so many years that I've gotten used to all sorts of mysterious sounds, but this one was very puzzling. What could it be?

Last winter I was kept awake for nights on end by a nasty, ripping sound under the roof. It turned out to be a family of squirrels making a nest in the rather expensive insulation we'd just installed in the attic.

Now that it's gotten cold again, and the heat's back on, more interesting noises are being heard around the house. When I shuffled into the kitchen yesterday morning to console myself with a strong cup of coffee, I was fascinated, although a little dismayed, to discover the source of the latest disturbance: All of the new wallpaper your company put up last week has snapped off the walls and rolled right up to the ceiling. It looks very odd. Maybe something went wrong with the paste?

The president of the company was so relieved to be treated without hostility by an unhappy client that he offered to install new wallpaper immediately—free of charge. "Thanks for being so decent about the bloody paper," he was reported to have said. "I can't tell you how awful most clients would have been. . . . Is there anything we can do about your bathrooms?"

A Little Quiet Diplomacy

Sometimes a phone call, or even a long, personal conversation just can't do the job of resolving a difference of opinion. Under these circumstances it is often best to formalize your point of view and define your objectives in a letter. The trick is to be clear and firm without injuring the other person's feelings or insulting their sensibilities. Humor rarely hurts, and sometimes a little mild self-effacement can go a long way toward leveling the ground and putting your correspondent at ease.

Jane Austen once had to devise a delicate way of discouraging an acquaintance, James Stanier Clarke, from making suggestions about the kinds of books she should write. Austen understood that Clarke's intentions were friendly and well-meant, but as a very independent-minded writer, she felt it necessary to inform him that she had no other choice but to "go her own way":

My dear Sir,

. . . You are very, very kind in your hints as to the sort of composition which might recommend me at present, and I am fully sensible that an historical romance, founded on the House of Saxe-Coburg, might be much more to the purpose of profit or popularity than such pictures of domestic life in country villages as I deal in—but I could no more write a romance

than an epic poem. I could not sit seriously down to write a serious romance under any other motive than to save my life, and if it were indispensable for me to keep it up and never relax into laughing at myself or other people, I am sure I should be hung before I had finished the first chapter. No, I must keep to my own style and go on in my own way; and though I may never succeed again in that, I am convinced that I should totally fail in any other.

I remain, my dear Sir,

Your very much obliged, and very sincere friend,

J. Austen

Making a Friendly Connection

The old maxim that "people like to be treated like people," no matter how important they are, is true. Imagine how disappointed and bored elected officials, magazine editors, and corporate employers must be when they receive so many dull, self-conscious, and overly reverent letters. But it's not always our fault. Sometimes we get so tongue-tied just thinking about how powerful and influential the person is to whom we're writing, that we can't express ourselves in a natural way. It's hard to think of a letter as "a visit on paper," when the person you're writing to spends all her time on Capitol Hill or runs a Fortune 500 company; nor is it any easier to envision letter-writing as "just talking on paper" when you've never had a real conversation with her either. No matter.

The point of any letter is to make a friendly connection, and the best way to do that is to think of the person to whom you are writing as a friend. Your composure, good humor, and interesting thoughts will be restored as soon as you focus on what you want to say, not on how to say it. Relax, speak as you would normally, and use your own words. The conversational "patter" of your ordinary speech will give your letter a more natural sound. At the same time, you'll be surprised to discover that for all its warmth and interest your letter won't sound any less "professional" than a more decorous one.

Well-written working letters do more than simply engage the interest of those who read them; they have the power to influence people and can give you opportunities to do the things you've always dreamed of doing. After a satisfying interview with an influential editor at a major book publishing company, a friend spent an entire weekend agonizing over whether or not she should write a thank-you note to her interviewer. She worried that it would look pushy or sound presumptuous. Finally, she sat down and fired off a short, sincere message, thanking the editor for a stimulating and exciting hour of conversation. Toward the end of the note she couldn't resist adding a personal thought: "I was moved and flattered that you took so much time to get to know me. Thank you." Neatly handwritten on heavy, cream-colored notepaper, her letter looked and sounded just as poised and confident as she herself had been during the interview. Not surprisingly, she received a call back from the editor, requesting a second interview.

There is really no trick to making important connections, or any need to agonize over them. Just trust your instincts about people and act on them as graciously as possible. Even the most hard-working letter is a gift of yourself . . . and if there is anything to be gained from such a letter, why shouldn't it be friendship?

Dear Reader,

   We've come to the end of our letter to you, and can think of no better way to say good-bye than to quote the words of Emily Dickinson:

My letter as a bee, goes laden.
Please love us and remember us.
Please write us very soon, and
tell us how you are. . . .

Permissions

Write Back
Soon!